THE
DIEGO
MASCIAGA

≈ WAY ≈

THE
DIEGO
MASCIAGA
~ WAY ~

LESSONS FROM THE MASTER OF
CUSTOMER SERVICE

CHRIS PARKER

urbanepublications.com

First published in Great Britain in 2014
by Urbane Publications Ltd
Suite 3, Brown Europe House, 33/34 Gleamingwood Drive,
Chatham, Kent ME5 8RZ

ISBN 978-1-909273-48-1

Design and Typeset by Julie Martin

Printed in Great Britain by
CPI Group (UK) Ltd,
Croydon, CR0 4YY

urbanepublications.com

April 2015

'It isn't a job, it's a life.'

Diego Masciaga

To Ruth and Willfred,

"Service is Pleasing,

~~Kindest~~ Regards

Diego

Dedication

Diego

Firstly, I dedicate this book about my life's work to my wonderful wife, Kerry, and my beautiful daughters Francesca and Isabella. They are unique. They have supported me in all ways possible, even though I work very long, unsociable hours and am not with them as much as we would all like. They always make sure that I go to work in a good mood and that I return to a happy home. They even try to disguise how much they miss me. Without their unwavering support I could not have achieved all that I have. They are my trade secret. They are my family. I love them.

Secondly, I would like to dedicate this to my parents, my mum, Anna, and dad, Pierino, for teaching me the importance of humility and modesty and, most importantly, for teaching me how to take pleasure in giving. They instilled in me the right attitudes, high standards of performance, and a great work ethic. Through their example they taught me about the gift – and the power – of Service. I can never repay them.

Chris

For me this book, like every other book, like everything else, is for "M". My life condensed into one letter.

FOREWORDS

Diego is a unique person. He inspires admiration and accolades the world over, yet whenever I look at the great man, think about him or greet him, he is always "my Diego". I cannot imagine my life without him and he is as crucial to the success of The Waterside Inn as the food served therein. Quite simply, Diego was born to please, a rare vocation. He should be called "un marchand de bonheur", since he finds life-fulfilling pleasure in his sense of duty to make people happy. In fact, service is not a career for Diego, *it is* him.

There is a particular satisfaction to be had from doing something right and Diego always does his inimitable best. He can be seen every day, excitedly awaiting lunch and dinner service, like a great actor before he takes the stage, the maestro ready to give another great performance, as inspired and fresh as if it was his first day. Yet his sense of humility, dignity and service is recognised and therefore he is trusted. Royalty, celebrities, newcomers and regulars alike, from all walks of life, are treated to the same equanimity, the same beaming, radiant smile and gracious welcome.

I first witnessed him in action in 1985 at Le Mazarin restaurant in Pimlico, one of the restaurants my brother Albert and I owned, and where Diego was in charge of the

Dining Room. As I watched him work, I knew he would be perfect to lead the Front of House at The Waterside Inn, a role he took on at last in 1988. My favourite experience at The Waterside Inn is to see Diego carving duck or a baron d'agneau, or preparing un homard ā la nage and being able to plate it in less than 2 minutes, a breath-taking feat.

In my travels to every corner of the globe, there is always the same question, "How is Diego"? He is held in extraordinary affection the world over. His leadership has inspired hundreds of young people to progress careers in the hospitality and catering industry.

There is so much more I want to say about my Diego, it could fill another book. I consider him as my son and I am so proud of him – but you will have to read on to discover in these pages more about his true love. It's an extraordinary privilege for you to meet not just a person, but the exemplar of quality that is Diego.

Michel Roux, O.B.E., Global Ambassador,
The Waterside Inn

Because I'm in the cooking business it can happen that, when I go out to eat with friends and family, the staff give me the lion's share of the attention and everyone else misses out.

With Diego, things are different.

When we went to the Waterside for my birthday a couple of years ago, he paid generous attention to every person at the table – all the while spooning caviar into our bowl of pasta with exactly the right amount of showmanship and panache. Just when you thought he'd finished, he'd spoon in yet another dollop. And another. He knew exactly what he was doing and had us all in the palm of his hand.

This is what makes Diego such an exceptional maître d'. He's friendly and considerate and will make you feel like the most important people in the restaurant. He exudes warmth and energy and has complete control of the dining room, but does so in such a way that staff and diners alike feel completely relaxed. And he has that deft sense of theatre that can turn a meal into an experience.

All of which makes him the perfect person to write a book about working front-of-house. *The Diego Masciaga Way* gives invaluable insights into what it takes and how it's done. And it's an engaging, inspiring portrait of a true professional and showman.

Heston Blumenthal

TESTIMONIALS

"Why do I love Diego Masciaga? I believe in Italian hospitality...Under the teaching received from Albano Mainardi (leader of the Italian art of hospitality and founder of the great Scuola Professionale Alberghiera E. Maggia di Stresa), students have learnt to respect its "rules" and precision, and bring the real Italian hospitality into the world...Diego Masciaga is the "Master" of this. I still remember the smiling expression of a young joyful student ready to learn a difficult and hard profession. Diego was only 15 years old. It was 1978, and he was starting his splendid career at the E.Maggia school. For me, he is the perfect example of a young professional positively pursuing his own journey toward an ultimate goal, constantly learning in prestigious environments with inspirational teachers, from the Hotel Royal of La Baule (chêne Lucien Barrière) to The Waterside Inn. Diego Masciaga has been able to interpret real customer service. He can communicate feelings, evoke memories, surprise the guest; and prepare his staff to be the best, teaching the vital importance of a smile, style and elegance. The skill of Diego Masciaga is a demonstration of the pinnacle of the profession – a capacity to express, with a very personal and unique touch, the poetry of Service. That's why I love Diego Masciaga."

Alberto Gozzi, Presidente HOSPES "La Scuola di Stresa"

"My family and I have been visiting the Waterside for over 20 years. We celebrated winning the Rugby World Cup with friends at the Waterside in 2003. It never ceases to amaze me and at the centre of all is Diego. As well as enjoying the most wonderful meal and experience, I love to watch Diego's team at work; it is a perfect example of a high performing team. The way in which the team coordinate their roles throughout the course of a lunch or dinner is like watching a choreographed dance. It's often struck me how a team in a kitchen and front of house such as the Waterside is no different to an elite sports team. It is their ability to operate at a high level when under pressure that the Waterside does so well which is the key characteristic of any high performing team. This level of attainment starts at the top and is due to the standards and culture set by those in Leadership positions. Diego understands and epitomises this better than anybody else with his uncompromising approach and legendary attention to detail. This book is a must read for anybody who is interested in delivering exceptional performance."

Sir Clive Woodward, Founder & Chairman of Captured

"Diego Masciaga, a Master in his field! For me, Diego epitomises the essence of fine service. It is not just his great charm and presence, nor his ability to lead, train and inspire those that work with him, but at the heart of it all, it is Diego's deep sense of caring and belief in the will to please and the achievement of nothing less than perfection, consistently all day, every day!"

Edward Griffiths CVO, Deputy Master of the Royal Household

"The thing about Diego is that he perfectly represents one of the main reasons why The Waterside has consistently been rated as one of the world's best restaurants. You can't separate Diego from the food in that they both represent the perfect dining experience. I have known him for as long as he has worked at The Waterside and sometimes take great delight in watching him work the room, forever charming without being ingratiating, attentive without ever becoming obsequious. It's like watching a great actor at work except you sense Diego is not working to a script but relying instead on an intuitive definition of what service should be. A remarkable man and a remarkable story to tell."

Sir Michael Parkinson, broadcaster, author and journalist

"Lasting memories are created from those first impressions and I have always been taken by the welcome and greeting every customer receives from Diego Masciaga when dining at The Waterside Inn, Bray. Diego is the Master at making sure every customer feels like they are the most important guest of the night. He serves his customers in a way that lets them know from the outset that they are the most important people in his world. Add to this a truly "genuine" tone to his attention and you have what can only be described as having come into contact with "THE GENERAL" when it comes to Customer Service. No one, anywhere does it better than Diego."

Peter Jones CBE, entrepreneur, business leader and presenter

"When we visit a great restaurant we understand that it will have a superb kitchen and highly talented and ambitious chefs. When we arrive, the way we are welcomed, the atmosphere, the surroundings, the theatre, the smooth effortlessness of the service – are all created and conducted by the maître d'hôtel. These combined with fabulous food create a beautiful memory. When I think of the warmest welcome, the best service, the pinnacle of hospitality, I think of Diego Masciaga. He is the greatest maître d'hôtel I know. He is an inspiration to all of us in the hospitality world and he is a wonderful man. I thoroughly recommend his book to all students of hospitality and indeed anyone involved in service."

Alastair Storey, Chairman of hospitality business WSH

"Diego is the Master of Service! If you want to know what Service is all about read this book!"

Silvano Giraldin, Director, Le Gavroche

"They don't award Michelin stars for service, nor for maître d's, but they should. For it's not only the food, nor the cooking, that makes a great restaurant. Ambience, décor, location all play their part in the making of a restaurant, but the most important ingredient is not the brilliance of the cuisine nor the wine list. It's the service that really makes the difference between enjoyment, and somewhere that brings you back to the table, again and again. The popularity of The Waterside is a testament to that quality of service, epitomized by its maître d', Diego Masciaga. A master of his craft, in every sense, as a teacher, a leader, an inspiration to his staff, and most importantly, a gracious, welcoming and ever-smiling host to his customers. Diego stands alone, worthy of not a mere three stars, but a constellation..."

Sir Terry Wogan, broadcaster and presenter

"Diego is the consummate restaurateur and one of the most respected in the UK. He was trained by one of the best, Mr Silvano Giraldin of Le Gavroche, to become one of the best. The Waterside Inn has been a favourite of my wife Eileen and I, and we have celebrated many birthdays, anniversaries and just great times in this idyllic location with their wonderful food. But what keeps us coming back is Diego's smiling face, charm and expertise in the art of service, which is the real reason we love it so much. It has always been my opinion that the manager sets the style, ambience and service levels of a restaurant and The Waterside Inn has all of these in abundance."

Geoffrey A. Gelardi, Managing Director,
The Lanesbrough

CONTENTS

ACKNOWLEDGEMENTS

Diego

These acknowledgements are for the great people in my profession who have all helped me to become 'Diego'.

From a very young age I was privileged to be taught by Commendatore Alberto Gozzi, one of the greatest in the profession of customer Service in Italy. He taught me that to be a great manager, you also have to gain general knowledge from many other fields, learn different languages and learn about different cultures. Three years ago Mr Gozzi sent me a personal letter telling me, 'l'allievo ha superato il maestro' (the pupil has surpassed the master). I cannot say how much that meant to me.

Mr Silvano Giraldin, GM and Director at Le Gavroche. This name doesn't need any introduction in the world of fine dining. The greatest restaurant manager, but also the kindest and most generous person I have met in my professional career, Mr Silvano taught me not only the art of Service, but more so the management, the administration and all that a manager needs to run a successful establishment. As the best teacher that a young person could have, he also taught me how to deal with problems and how to solve them without any repercussion.

Mr Michel Roux, OBE – the man who has allowed me to become 'Diego'. Even when I left his employ in 1994 and worked in Italy for eight months, he welcomed me back like a father. He has entrusted me for many, many years and every day he has been my alarm clock. The man, who despite being a great chef and a godfather of our industry, has been my mentor and guardian angel. Every day for 30 years.

Finally, a gentleman who spotted me many years ago on my 'football pitch' – his name is Chris Parker, the writer of this book. Chris has been able to enter my mind and bring out onto paper my personality, my philosophy about Service, my principles, my skills and the ways I apply them. This must have been extremely difficult as I am spontaneous by nature and not used to talking about myself. His 'ink' reminds me – and shows everyone – how important this profession is.

Thank you all.

Chris

I would like to thank my colleagues and friends at Nottingham Trent University for their continued support.

A special 'Thank you', of course, goes to Diego and all at The Waterside Inn, who have accepted my repeated intrusions into their world with grace and generosity.

Finally, my sincere thanks to Matthew Smith, the genius behind Urbane Publications. My work always benefits from his many skills. I benefit from his trust. One day, I am sure, he will pay for the drinks.

INTRODUCTION

You don't always have to travel to find treasure. You do have to dig.

I first spoke to Diego Masciaga, Master of Customer Service, Restaurant Manager and Director of the 3 Michelin starred restaurant The Waterside Inn, by phone on a Friday afternoon in April 2010. I was planning a book about how to create and sustain business excellence based on a study of a select handful of restaurants and I wanted to know if The Waterside Inn would take part.

We spoke for longer than I had expected. Diego agreed to take part in the project, subject to the support of his employers, the Roux family. We met some months later. He was charming, astute, and generous. These qualities come naturally to him. His reputation as one of the greatest restaurant managers on the planet is, however, the result of decades of un-ending commitment, learning and leadership.

Before finishing that original book, which was published under the title *Five Essential Ingredients for Business Success*, I knew I wanted to pursue a second, even more specific study. I needed to explore and come to understand precisely how Diego Masciaga creates and provides some of the best customer Service experienced anywhere in the world.

I've been a student, practitioner and teacher of intra- and inter-personal communications and influence since the mid 1970s. Customer Service has always been a fascination. I understand how the use of words and the manner and timing of their delivery can create and change a person's emotional state. I recognise how body language shares myriad messages. I know that if you want to influence irresistibly you absolutely have to recognise the other person's starting point and meet them there. I was convinced that these and other interpersonal skills, when combined with relevant technical abilities and supportive systems and processes, could produce outstanding Service.

I was convinced; I had simply failed to meet the person who proved it.

I had come, therefore, to think of outstanding customer Service as the most precious of buried treasure. I believed in its existence – there had been enough glimpses along the way to keep the belief alive – but no matter where I travelled I found myself digging in the wrong places.

Until I met Diego Masciaga.

The more I observed Diego and his team in action, the more I questioned, tested and challenged them, the more I earned his trust, the more I came to realise that the treasure I had been seeking was here – in safe hands and hearts.

With Diego's permission I returned repeatedly. I recorded everything. I came to understand his approach to exceptional customer care. It is based on a philosophy, built around principles and perfected through practice. It is shared through processes with no purpose other than to make Service as easy, effective and wonderful as possible.

This book explains them all. It provides the essentials for creating the very best customer Service. It focuses on attitude, aptitude and adaptability, caring and consistency, passion, performance and purpose, interaction and intention. It has nothing do with the use of automated response systems, the completion of computer-generated checklists, rigid un-thinking adherence to routines, or scripted replies quoted by all.

It is, rather, a book about how best to manage the imme-diacy of working with your customers to achieve only the most positive of outcomes. It acknowledges the many challenges that litter the path to customer Service excellence. It provides the solutions. It offers a multitude of truths. All hard earned and consistently proven by one man over decades of being the very best at what he does.

This is a book that shares the lessons from my many, very inspiring conversations with a Master of customer Service.

Ralph Waldo Emerson wrote, '*Truth is the property of no individual but is the treasure of all men*'. The lessons we can learn from Diego Masciaga are valuable treasure indeed.

Take them. Apply them. Share them. If you do, we will all benefit.

Chris

1

SERVICE

The Essence

∾

> *'The essence of all beautiful art, all great art, is gratitude.'*
> Frederick Nietzsche

The first question

'It is very difficult,' Diego Masciaga says as we sit in The Waterside Inn's summerhouse, 'to write or even talk about Service, because each guest is different and so each Service is also different. Service is...'

He pauses, looking out at the river as he seeks the best way to answer the question I asked a moment ago, 'Just what is Service?'

Another moment slips by. In my notes I write,

He's wrestling to pin down the necessary explanation.

Only with the benefit of distance and hindsight, I know that I was wrong. He wasn't wrestling. He was putting a loving arm around the difficulty of explaining the practice – the *art* – to which he has dedicated his life.

'Service,' he says again, 'Is so difficult to put into words...'

And yet there we were. Seeking to do just that, to find the right words. To write a book, *this* book, about Diego Masciaga's approach to creating exemplary customer Service. To write about just what Service is and how you measure and maintain it. And why it *matters*. And why something matters is far more than just its purpose. After all, every structure, system or process within an organisation should have a purpose.

Some things, though, matter far more than others. Some things matter more because they can achieve a multitude of purposes and, far more importantly, because we give them emotional power. We find ourselves being moved by these things. We commit ourselves to them. We create a relationship with them. We give them meaning and this meaning, in turn, becomes one of those significant factors by which we come to define ourselves.

Service is one of these things. It is real and powerful and recognisable – often by its absence – and as hard to describe accurately as any emotion. Service has its purposes, of course. Done well, it creates significant personal and corporate outcomes. It is at the heart of customer satisfaction. Actually, at its very best it is the source of customer delight. It significantly increases the likelihood of repeat business.

It is a powerful corporate USP. It feeds the bottom line.

Everyone knows the importance of Service. Many trumpet their commitment and ability to provide it brilliantly.

For thirty minutes – the space between writing the last line and writing this one – I looked at twenty-four business websites at random. 90 per cent of them promised outstanding customer Service. And yet recent research estimates that businesses in the UK lose £12 billion every year[1] as a result of poor customer Service and that inadequate Service can cost brands as much as one fifth of their annual revenue.

This is not surprising when the *People 1st's 2010 State of the Nation report* revealed that 65 per cent of businesses acknowledged staff were lacking the necessary customer Service skills. It's not surprising when the report, *Global Insights on Succeeding in the Customer Experience Era*, revealed that whilst 93 per cent of business executives said that improving customer experience was one of their top priorities, 37 per cent of companies were only just beginning to put formal customer experience initiatives in place, and a mere 20 per cent considered their customer experience initiatives to be 'advanced'.

If the legendary broadcaster Sir David Attenborough had chosen to seek out and report on exceptional Service instead of the world's most rare wildlife, he would have made far fewer documentaries.

---

1 Businesses in the USA lose over $40 billion.

The message is: **Trust the research and not the website promises**.

The question is: **If everyone knows the importance of great Service, why are so few organisations or individuals providing it?**

Especially when research also reveals that, after receiving good Service, 71 per cent of customers will then recommend the business to others and 44 per cent will use it more frequently.

The answer is two-fold. The first takes us back to Diego Masciaga, the Master, staring thoughtfully at the River Thames and searching for the right words with which to answer my question. It takes us back to the very nature of Service itself.

To Diego, Service is more than a corporate necessity[2]. Service is primarily a calling, a cause, an emotional compulsion that cannot be refused. Whilst its existence might be dependent on appropriate systems and structures, whilst it might be revealed through the constant application of a variety of skills, Service is born out of an overwhelming desire, an insatiable need, to serve.

For Diego Masciaga, Service matters because, he says finally, his gaze still fixed on the river, his words as much an

---

2 Although he absolutely recognises its business value.

The Diego Masciaga Way

affirmation to himself as they are an answer to me, 'Serving is pleasing.'

For this man, only the third ever recipient of the Grand Prix de l'Art de la Salle, an award given by the L'Académie Internationale de Gastronomie to those acknowledged as the greatest restaurant managers alive, it is as simple and as complex as that.

Service is pleasing.

It is simple because it is only a three-word answer and they are all every day, non-technical words. It is complex because, as Diego makes clear through his explanation, his example and the behaviour and attitudes of his staff, Service is both a verb and a noun.

It is a verb because customer Service is most obviously a process, an interaction that takes place between professionals and customers. Epiah Khan, the apocryphal Persian mystic, wrote, 'Reality exists in the space between two people'. Whether that is true or not, we can say for certain that the reality of customer Service is experienced within that space.

Service, the Diego Masciaga way, is the result of the skilled understanding, on-going recognition of, and speedy response to, the ever-changing needs of every individual customer, combined with the application of unique technical skills and the management of environments and atmosphere.

Service is produced by well-motivated, well-trained teams

that understand and value the various outcomes that Service creates. Importantly, they also know that the most immediate outcome, that which exists in the space between people, determines to what extent the other outcomes are achieved. Simply put,

Pleasing leads to profit.

It leads to the very obvious financial profit achieved through increased business and to the very personal profit of pleasure in making others happy.

'Service begins with a genuine smile,' Diego says, unconsciously touching his heart as he speaks. 'Staff must be happy to serve. They must be truly grateful for the opportunity to do so. If they provide exceptional Service they might even be rewarded twice – by their own sense of pleasure and by the customer's gratitude.'

Interestingly, Diego also refers to this gratitude-fuelled process, these inevitably influential interactions, as a noun. He talks of Service as an entity that is at once there to be valued, worked for, longed for, whilst simultaneously being tantalisingly just out of reach in its most perfect form.

I write in my notes,

Diego Masciaga has committed himself to the service of Service. It is his life's mission.

For its part, he tells me, Service rewards loyalty by

demanding more. It repays commitment by offering glimpses of its perfect Self and encouraging – *daring* – you to come even closer. And if you have the courage, if you care enough to accept the challenge, perfect Service rewards your efforts by always requiring just that little bit more, true perfection remaining just out of reach.

There is always more of me, it seems to say. *I am here to be strived for, never reached. I expect you to keep striving though, no matter what the personal cost. I expect you to make people happy. Always. With gratitude. Do you understand?*

Diego Masciaga understands. I am getting my first insights. This is why it is easier to make promises on a website than to actually deliver exceptional customer care. Service is far more than a series of agreed responses or behaviours. It requires much more than technical knowledge or skill. It isn't measured by a tick list.

If you don't enjoy making people happy, if you are not grateful for the opportunity to create wonderful experiences for others that will live on and be shared as treasured memories, if the thought of doing that doesn't spark a genuine smile on your face, then don't bother with Service. Stay well away. For your own sake and that of others. Service demands a full-on, heart-felt, non-stop relationship. Nothing less will do.

This leads us on to the second reason why it is easier to promise great customer care than to actually deliver it;

the second reason why Diego Masciaga's ability to deliver outstanding Service is exceptional:

Service is a 24/7 commitment.

Diego smiles. Not the genuinely happy smile he offers guests, not a smile of welcome and gratitude. This is more layered than that, more introspective. This is a smile inspired by a lifetime of learning, by innumerable experiences. Diego looks away from the river for the first time in several minutes. He takes a sip of his espresso and then says, 'It isn't a job...it is a life.'

Of course it is. At least it's his life. Whether or not it is a life deliberately chosen or one shaped by an innate, irresistible instinct, I cannot say. Not yet. Right now Diego is keen to stress the intensity of the commitment required. The essence of success, he emphasises, lies not just in being able to create and provide outstanding Service, but in providing it repeatedly, day after day, year after year.

'Anyone can be great for a few days,' he concludes quietly.

And so the second fold is reinforced. Like a world champion sportsman, the struggle to become the best is replaced by the even greater struggle to remain the best. Diego has been living this struggle – staying at the top of the global customer Service ladder – for nearly three decades.

I write,

Where does his stamina come from?

Then I realise that he has already told me. It comes from his commitment to the service of Service. When he says, 'It isn't a job, it's a life,' he actually means that, for him, it is a *way* of life.

The paradox lies in the fact that, as I have already discovered, for Diego Service is a verb as well as a noun, and yet Service does not exist in its own right. People create it. The word 'Service' is just a way of identifying specific types of human interaction. The truth is that Diego is both the creator and the follower of the notion of Service that he has been describing to me. He has absolute control over it. Yet he talks to me as if he does not. The ever-changing, always just out of reach, perfect Service that he aspires to is actually a product of his own imagination. It is the product of his constant striving and learning. It is Diego himself who keeps redefining the ideal, who fuels his own stamina by ensuring that he has to keep moving forward.

I suspect that on one level he knows this. I am sure, though, that he keeps this understanding buried deep in his subconscious. It must be far easier, I realise, for a man who loves to serve to find the motivation and the energy to be the best through a belief in something distinct from himself. It makes sense for that type of person to think and talk of Service as a noun first and foremost.

I note quickly,

That's it! That's why he is committed to the service of Service! The very act of serving energises him! He keeps going – keeps getting better – because he isn't doing it for himself. He isn't even doing it just for the people he serves. He's doing it in honour of an ideal he believes in. It reflects his world-view. This is *who* he is, not just *what* he does.

As I stop writing the words of Elbert Hubbard, the American artist, writer and philosopher, pop into my mind. They feel immediately at home as I sit here next to Diego Masciaga in the summerhouse by the Thames, whilst around us his team prepare quietly and efficiently for yet another restaurant sitting. Hubbard wrote, 'Art is not a thing – it is a way.'

It is a view I have always shared. Only now, based on what Diego has said, I find myself asking an unexpected question, is Service a form of art? After all, I have already accepted that what I have found here at The Waterside Inn is a *way* of Service – a philosophy and a discipline, the pursuit of an ideal that is heart-felt and business-wise, that reflects beliefs and values and shapes behaviours. I'm already starting to consider the notion that Service is somehow bigger, more important, than the individuals who provide it.

I return to my first question and challenge myself with it.

Q: 'Just what is Service?'
A: Service is ethereal and tangible. It is a cause in the most powerful, emotional, compelling meaning of the word. It is a corporate necessity that simply cannot afford to be soulless.

Q: So just what is Service?

A: Pleasing...

I'm not sure if I want to draw a smiley face next to that or my version of Munch's *The Scream*. I do believe what I have written. I know what I have felt when experiencing Service at the hands of Diego and his team. It's just that somehow I'm struggling to pin it down precisely on paper. But then again, he did warn me that I would.

We have another thirty minutes together before it is time for lunch. Time enough for one more question. I know in which direction I need to go next. If I am going to make any more sense of the emotional compulsion that drives Diego Masciaga's pursuit of the Service ideal, and of that ideal itself, I have to go back in time. I have to discover how and why it began. And why he couldn't let it go. Once I understand that then I can focus on how he creates, delivers and maintains the outstanding level of Service he is famous for.

The second question, then, 'Diego, how did it start?

The beginning

He was born in 1963 in Oleggio, a small village near Stresa in Italy. His inspiration was his mother. He is quick to explain, 'She taught me by her example about the importance of Service. Whenever I needed something, she was always there ahead of me. She always seemed to know what I needed before I had to ask.'

Thus inspired, the career path was set from an early age. The fourteen-year-old Diego began taking seasonal work at five star hotels in France and Italy. His instinct for Service was immediately obvious. The relationship between Service and profit revealed itself to him equally quickly.

'One of my first jobs was in a very prestigious hotel in La Baule on the west coast of France. The hotel was very popular with the Parisian aristocracy. Because of my youth and lack of experience I was allowed only to provide Service to children and dogs. At 5pm I had the food orders given to me for the many dogs staying in the rooms whilst their owners had dinner. I knew that if I got this wrong I would ruin the customers' holiday. I didn't want that. I wanted to play my part in making it wonderful for them. These people talked to me a lot and I listened very carefully. So I learnt many things. I also got more tips than anyone else! When guests left I would often give them a gift for their child or their dog. They appreciated that and the care I had given throughout very much!'

Diego's smile disappears. He leans forward almost conspiratorially. This wasn't, I realize, just a pleasant memory. There is a lesson here too. And he has to share it. It's the other essential part of his nature. He loves to teach. But maybe serving and teaching are not so far apart?

'You see,' Diego says, 'in business you have to be a great listener. If you don't listen you don't learn. When I listen I seek to *enter into* their conversation.'

I make a note,

The importance of listening – we'll come back to this.

At the age of seventeen Diego made the brave decision to leave home and move to France, to work in Alain Chapel's 3 Michelin starred restaurant. It was to be a challenging and lonely time for the young Italian. The world-famous restaurant, owned and run by a chef widely acknowledged as one of the greatest of his generation, was in the village of Mionnay, twelve miles outside Lyon. As an inexperienced Italian, Diego was not allowed to work in the restaurant during Service. Instead he was required only to organise the empty green and brown bottles ready for collection.

Living apart from his family for the first time in accommodation that was several miles away from the restaurant, Diego found the isolation and the long hours stressful. He talks of the many times he travelled back to his room in the early hours of a winter morning, struggling through the intense cold and the snow knowing he would be making the return journey in a few short hours. He admits that it was a time in which he cried often. His resolve was clearly tested and yet never beaten.

'My desire to learn,' Diego says without emotion, 'was always stronger than my tears.'

Alain Chapel took a liking to the determined young man and instructed him to serve lunch and dinner to the Chapel family every day before the guests arrived and Service began. It was at these times that the great chef rewarded Diego's desire to learn, personally teaching him the fine arts of serving and carving. As Diego's ability grew, so did his standing in the French restaurant.

He stayed there until 1983 when he moved to work for Albert and Michel Roux Snr. at the 3 Michelin starred Le Gavroche in London. He was promoted quickly to the role of Chef De Rang. Two years later he moved again, becoming the manager at Le Mazarin, another restaurant owned by the Roux brothers. It achieved a Michelin star within months of him taking charge. From there – following a relatively brief spell working for Michel Roux Snr. in California and a return to Alain Chapel's, this time as maître d' – Diego moved to The Waterside Inn in 1988.

Since then he has played a pivotal role in The Waterside Inn's success and established his reputation as one of the great restaurant managers of his generation.

As such, he has, by special request organised many private dinners and banquets. Occasionally he teaches Service skills at the Istituto-Professionale Alberghiero "E.Maggia" in Stresa and he is the holder of an Honorary Doctorate from this institution.

Not surprisingly, he has been winning awards and accolades for many years. In 2000 he was the winner of the Master of Culinary Arts, awarded by the Royal Academy of Culinary Arts. In 2007 he won the Maître de Maître award from the Academy of Food and Wine Society. A year later the same society named him Restaurant Manager of the Year. In 2011 he was honoured by his home country with the title of Cavaliere, the Italian equivalent of a knighthood, for his services to fine dining and his commitment to the development and training of others. In the National

Restaurant Awards 2014, The Waterside Inn received the prestigious Service Award.

Throughout it all, Diego assures me, the lesson he learnt from his mother has remained his core principle. He continues to measure the quality of the Service his team provides by asking himself, 'Are we pleasing our guests and meeting their needs before they are expressed?' For him, everything comes back to this.

'So', I say, 'Service means never having to ask?'

He nods. 'Absolutely. If the guest has to ask it means we have not been watching closely enough; we have not understood them well enough. You see, we are here to create contentment. As I have said, serving is all about pleasing people, making them feel happy and good, making them feel comfortable. This is true whether it is in a restaurant, a shop, a bank, even a call centre. It is true anywhere.'

*True anywhere...*At least it should be. I'm sure that is what he meant. Diego leaves me to lead another unique lunchtime Service.

I write my notes as follows,

Summary

Service is at once tangible and intangible. Just like every other human interaction it exists and disappears in the instant. Yet its effect is profound. It influences both the Service professional and those they are serving. Too often exceptional Service is noticeable by its absence. This is because Service excellence, as with all other forms of excellence, cannot be achieved through occasional study and practice. It is a full-time commitment.

The lessons are:

Lesson no. 1

Service is pleasing. It is about creating contentment and comfort. It is about making people feel happy and good.

Lesson no. 2

Service begins with a genuine smile. People who serve should have an emotional compulsion to do so. Service excellence can only be achieved and maintained by people who make an absolute commitment. It requires a willingness to learn continually. It also requires stamina.

Lesson no. 3

Every Service interaction is unique. It is a once-in-a-lifetime opportunity to create a wonderful experience for someone else. To achieve this staff have to recognise and respond speedily to the ever-changing needs of those they are serving.

Lesson no. 4

Pleasing leads to profit. Excellent Service creates repeat business. It creates great word-of-mouth publicity. It is a powerful and productive USP. It is essential for continual business growth.

As I review the above I decide there are four key areas I need to focus upon if I am going to identify fully how Diego Masciaga creates the outstanding levels of Service for which he has been so recognised.

These areas are:

~ Recruitment and staff training
~ Leadership and the importance of being a role model
~ Service delivery – understanding customers and meeting their needs
~ Ensuring longevity, consistency and creating improvement.

These will be the focus for the rest of this book.

~

2

RECRUITMENT & TRAINING

The 3 H's

∾

'Attitude not aptitude determines altitude.'
Zig Ziglar

Hunger, humility and honesty

Diego Masciaga is a well-dressed Italian with silver grey hair, a face that smiles easily, and eyes that occasionally reflect a hint of steel. He speaks several languages fluently, has an eye for detail and accepts no compromises when it comes to maintaining standards. He understands that the level of Service provided by any organisation is determined by three factors:

1) The quality of the staff employed and their individual and collegiate commitment to Service

2) The quality and nature of the training they receive

3) The ability of leaders within the organisation to act as inspiring role models, create a culture that prioritises Service excellence, and actively pursue ever-higher standards.

For Diego, outstanding Service begins with employing outstanding staff. And in this regard outstanding means those who stand out as having a passion – a *need* – to commit to the service of Service. It doesn't mean they have to be great at it already. This is why he takes personal responsibility for recruiting and training his team.

'I employ based on their attitude and their willingness to learn.'

He says this with such quiet yet total conviction it makes one immediately question the validity of any other approach. In fact, it was several meetings later before I finally challenged his presupposition.

'Diego, The Waterside Inn has held 3 Michelin stars for well over a quarter of a century. It's a world-renowned restaurant. Surely to maintain such levels of performance you have employ people with world-class skills?'

Now it is Diego's turn to study me for a moment. It is one of those rare occasions when I feel as if our roles have temporarily reversed. I suddenly get a brief insight into why he has always previously refused to be the focus of such detailed attention; why he still feels a degree of awkwardness – stress, even – before our meetings. I sense that he is trying to decide whether I actually mean what I have just said, or whether I am just testing him in some way.

Whatever decision he comes to, he replies as he so often does: slowly at first and then with increasing speed and passion, with instinctive gestures, a shift in posture and an obvious change of breath. This isn't the Diego who performs in the restaurant with charm and grace, sometimes with energy and exaggeration, sometimes with deliberately subdued thoughtfulness. *That* Diego is real and true. It is a vital part of the man. As important to him, I am sure, as it is to his guests. *This* Diego, however, is talking from a different place within himself, somewhere closer to the absolute source of who he is. Despite his self-admitted stress at being interviewed by me, he is once again doing what he has always done: sharing himself, allowing me access to the powerful, irresistible beliefs that have shaped his life and, because of his leadership, the lives of many within and beyond his industry.

He is, whether he realises it or not, providing another lesson. He is committing to a process – being analysed by me – which we both know he finds challenging, awkward and uncomfortable. When we meet like this Diego is the focus of my attention and he much prefers it when I, as the guest, am the focus of his. Yet he is responding to me with honesty, openness and integrity.

The lesson is: if you believe in something enough (and it needn't be Service, it can be anything) then you have to be willing to do those things you would otherwise walk away from. If you care you have to share, even if it makes your heart beat faster than it should. Diego Masciaga, I consider later, has been doing this for all of his adult life. That is why he is an industry leader, a Champion of Service. That's why I'm here.

'Having the right attitude,' Diego says, straightening slightly, 'is very important. Some people want the job so much you can feel it even when they talk to you on the phone. And at the end of the day attitude is what it is all about. If you don't have the right attitude, in any profession, you will never succeed. You have to be hungry – desperate – to succeed. We all know the technique and we can develop this through training. Anyone can learn these things. Technique is teachable. What I also teach, the most important thing, is to understand that serving is pleasing. It is far more than just knowing how to carve meat or select the best wine. It is far more than just technical ability or knowledge.'

This is from a man who has mastered all of the technical aspects of his role and whose knowledge of food and wine is exemplary. He clearly knows that these aspects matter, that in the grand scheme of things they play a vital part in ensuring that guests are at least satisfied. It is just that he regards them as in some way secondary to the Service attitude and aptitude of all staff. His philosophy seems to be that technical mistakes are easier to correct than Service errors, that no matter how good the product if the Service does not at least match it, customers will go elsewhere. In the final analysis Service is the glue that bonds the customer to the organisation. I check that I have understood him correctly. This time his response is swift.

'Of course. Think of it this way. Imagine that I want to buy a car and it is for sale in two different garages. In the first garage the Service is terrible. I can see that the sales person doesn't really care. They do not have a genuine smile. They are interested only in how much commission they can make. They don't really care about the car and they certainly don't care about pleasing me. So I go to the second garage. There the car is a little more expensive, but the person smiles from the heart. They listen to me carefully. They understand how to talk to me. They *connect* with me. Obviously, I am going to stay here. We will agree a sale. I will tell my friends how good the Service is. We will all be happy.'

I write in my notebook,

I am already hearing common mantras:

~ Serving is pleasing
~ Attitude comes first
~ Technique is teachable

I don't agree that Service begins with recruiting the right staff. I think he's missed something. I think he's taking something for granted. I'll address this later; when the time is right.

Right now I want to stay with his approach to recruitment for a little longer. 'Diego, how do you know when a person has the right attitude and a genuine willingness to learn? You say you can feel it when they talk to you, but surely it's more than just a gut instinct?'

'I do have an instinct. However, it is based on what I see and occasionally what I hear. The truth is if someone really wants the job you are offering – if they *really* want it no matter what the cost – they show it in their eyes or in their handshake, not necessarily in their words. Sometimes someone tells me how much they want to work for me and yet I can see in their expression that they don't really mean it. I do everything I can to make sure that I meet the people I employ. I would say that 90 per cent of the time this is what happens. If it is impossible to see them in person, I phone them. And I listen to them very carefully. If it is a young person, I might phone early in the morning – around 9.30am – because I know that many young people tend to sleep in if they are not working.' Diego chuckles. 'If I call early and the person is immediately bright and enthusiastic, I take that as a good sign. If they are grumpy or they don't adjust quickly to my call, well...' His voice trails off.

Behind my smile I'm thinking, the look on their face, their handshake, the sound of their voice, this is recruitment taken back to the most basic of basics. I'm sitting here in a centre of excellence and at the very core of the recruitment practice is Diego's ability to *read* the other person. There are no rounds of interviews, presentations, or psychometric testing. There is just this man and his ability to look and listen. He's backing himself to recognise their desire and their talent.

'Not just their talent,' he corrects when I put the point to him. 'And I need to see more than desire. I need to see hunger. You have to be hungry, really very hungry, if you want to be great at anything. It is as true with Service as it is with sport or business, or any other type of performance.'

'Excuse me – any other type of performance? Are you suggesting that Service is performance?'

'I'm not suggesting, Mr Parker. I am telling you very clearly. Everyone involved in delivering Service, no matter what industry they are in, should understand and know how to perform for their guests. It is something we might talk more about, perhaps?'

I nod and note in equal measure. Another insight into how he thinks. Actually it's far more than that, because how he thinks about Service is always translated into action. There is no divide between his beliefs, thoughts and actions with regard to what Service is and how to provide it brilliantly. He is completely congruent. I can't help but note,

Perhaps that's what Mastery is, an absolute congruency between beliefs and behaviour, between intention and achievement.

This is purely a personal note. I would never tell Diego that I regard him as a Master of his art. He certainly doesn't refer to himself in that way. And that seems appropriate, to me at least. I would be as cautious of a person who told me they were a Master, as I am of those website promises of great Service. So I keep my thoughts of Mastery to myself. It avoids embarrassment for us both. Besides, right now Diego is hungry to talk about other things. And I'm happy to share this particular feast.

'There are different levels of hunger,' he says. 'And there are different levels of appetite. Some people can seem really keen, but you can tell they will be quickly satisfied. Or that they do not truly have the appetite for what lies ahead.' He nods, briefly, with barely controlled urgency and then continues. 'I also need to see two other qualities that are vitally important if someone is to be great at Service.'

'And they are?'

'The first is humility.' Diego speaks as if he is savouring the word. This time he pauses as if giving me a chance to roll it around my mind if not my mouth.

'Humility?'

'It is impossible to be committed to Service without it.'

I have done my fair share of recruitment and selection. I've done the interviewing, written the job descriptions and the person specifications. I have never once listed Hunger and Humility as essential criteria.[3]

I decide to approach this notion of humility in a circumspect way. After all, I'm talking to a man who is one of the very best on the planet, if not *the* best, at what he does. Can you be world class and still be humble? Can you have the insatiable hunger necessary to strive to be that good, and to then keep getting better, without an unshakeable belief

---

3 To be fair, I've never listed them as desired criteria either.

The Diego Masciaga Way

in your own capability? Does that belief swamp humility? It certainly doesn't seem to in Diego's case. Still, sometimes it's best to tread softly...

'Diego, you've told me how you went to work in grand hotels as a teenager and then how you moved to France to work with Alain Chapel, what was your goal back then?'

The answer comes almost immediately as if it is a recent rather than a distant memory.

'My goal at the age of 16 was one day to be the restaurant manager of a famous restaurant. At Alain Chapel I learnt of Michelin stars. So then I wanted to be the restaurant manager of a 3 Michelin starred restaurant. At the beginning I had the choice of focussing on restaurants or hotels. I chose restaurants because I like the contact with people.'

'So you set the very highest targets for yourself?'

'If someone says to me, "I'm happy to be the fifth best..."' Diego shrugs. 'Well, of course, we want to be the best. But I never worked hard because I wanted to be able to say that I was number one. I worked hard to do the best I could. I just kept working and learning. I just kept challenging myself. Even now I am doing the same things. Learning never stops. I believe that if you always do your best, if you work hard, and if you do this consistently over a long period of time, the recognition and the awards come to you. That is really my advice to staff – just work hard to be your best and eventually good things will come. I want people who are hungry for success because they want to grow themselves – not just for money. Money too easily ruins hunger and humility.'

Two thoughts fight for dominance in my mind. They are both realisations. It's enough to give a man of my age a headache. It seems only fair, though. We have been talking about the inevitability of suffering for your art.

The first realisation is that if there is any domain in which brilliance and humility are an essential coupling it is Service. This is the domain that is all about someone else, the domain in which brilliance is measured by how others feel, by their experience and perspective. Service, The Diego Masciaga way, is all-but invisible and means never having to ask, so brilliance here cannot appeal to individuals who need their skill to be emphasised in the spotlight. What an interesting, inspiring and apparently contradictory motivation:

I want to be great at delivering Service. I want to be world-class – and if I manage to become brilliant you will never, ever, notice how hard I'm working or all the skills I have, because you will be too busy having a wonderful time.

The second realisation is that the vast majority of Diego's staff are young adults. They belong in the demographic known as Millennials. Of late, there has been much research and debate about whether or not Millennials have a more limited work ethic than older generations. Ignoring it all, Diego is, through his recruitment and training, developing young people with an outstanding – to use his words – *hunger* for work. Not only that, they are completely at ease living in the various depths of shadow that the restaurant hierarchy creates.

The Waterside Inn, like the other great restaurants I have studied, is militaristic in its use of hierarchy and role boundaries. It is militaristic in the way of the most elite military units who work best in the shadows, who strive to have only their outputs, rather than their processes, noticed. It is similar too in that its reputation for excellence precedes it. Diego has already made the point that not everyone who thinks they can manage the challenges and the pressure here actually can. The ideal recruit is both technically skilled and has an insatiable appetite for learning and performing. I am starting to understand though, why Diego emphasises attitude over ability. I write,

> You can't be elite unless you really, really want it, unless you are really willing to pay. And it isn't a one-off payment.

I realise suddenly that Diego is waiting patiently for my next question. I glance at my notes to distract me from my thoughts.

'You said there were two other qualities you needed to see. After humility what is the other one?'

'Honesty. Let me give you an example. If I offer someone a job and they tell me that, although they are employed, they won't worry about giving notice to their employer, they will find that my job offer is suddenly no longer there! Because I know that one day they will do the same thing to me. They should respect their employer and work their notice. This happened to me once. Many years ago I helped a young man in my team get the new job that he was ready for. As you know, this is an important part of my role. This young man, though, left The Waterside without working his notice. So I had a conversation with the person who had offered him the post. The young man arrived to begin his new job only to find that it had gone! Years later he sent me a letter apologising for his behaviour and saying "Thank you" for the lesson. Since then I have continued to help him.'

Of course he has. It is easy to imagine the long arm of Diego reaching out to slam a door shut, to teach a stern lesson, but it is even easier to imagine that same arm opening doors, providing guidance and support for as long as it is required. It is becoming clear that for Diego recruitment and training are brothers-in-arms, united by a bond that continues indefinitely. As already noted, when it comes to training and teaching Diego cannot help himself. His instinct is undeniable. He has to do it. His belief is that, once recruited, even the best of staff need both training and leadership if Service excellence is to be achieved and then maintained.

Recognising this, it is time for me to step away from recruitment and explore his approach to staff training. Not surprisingly, it is built around a simple mantra that reflects depths of integrity and commitment:

Train little by little, day by day

It is a mantra that, like all the others, Diego puts into practice unceasingly. It is integral to the high standards of Service he creates.

Why the buck stops and training doesn't

For Diego, the fact that excellence results from continual training is a simple and yet demanding truth. It is demanding because someone has to assume responsibility for providing that training. By extension, therefore, they are assuming responsibility for the quality of Service provided. In Diego's eyes the Service buck stops with the leader who accepts that responsibility. At The Waterside Inn the buck stops with him. And he wouldn't have it any other way.

Whenever I have modelled excellence – studied the beliefs, attitudes, thought processes and behaviours of those individuals acknowledged at being the very best at what they do – I've found they all possess an inner drive, a compulsion, to pursue their chosen path. It becomes impossible to separate the person from their particular practice. *It* is an integral part of their psychological make-up. Interestingly, too, *it* always seems obvious to them, certainly far more obvious than it does to the rest of us. It is as if they have been born with, or subconsciously developed, an unusual degree of insight into what it takes to make *it* brilliant. Not surprisingly, they also all have an enormous capacity for exertion and effort in pursuit of their goals.

Diego Masciaga shares these traits in abundance. He

has achieved the highest levels of professional excellence because he has developed his innate abilities over decades of study, self-sacrifice and un-ending hard work. Yet he also has the patience and understanding of an experienced and committed teacher.

'Teaching,' he says to me, 'is not just done formally. It is done through daily conversations. It is done by being a role model.'

'In that case,' I ask, 'is there ever a time when you are with your team and you are not either formally or informally teaching or modelling how you want them to behave?'

'Never.'

His smile suggests gratitude for my question. As if he is especially pleased for the opportunity to share this particular secret. The smile suggests also, I sense, a degree of fatigue. The sort of almost constant ache that is well known and understood – appreciated even – only by those who consistently push themselves to the limit. The sort of fatigue that becomes a reassuring friend, a confirmation of your expenditure, a powerful and most personal indicator of your willingness to pay any price in pursuit of your ideal.

Diego, of course, is not only driving himself to the limit, he is also leading – sometimes, perhaps, pushing – his team to the very edge of their capabilities, too. It is a significant, complex and undoubtedly draining responsibility.

'I train my team little by little, day by day,' he says. 'I can never rest from this whenever I am with them in the workplace. I have to follow them every day, talk to them, observe them, and teach them to think like me.'

I note without pause or subtlety,

...teach them to think like me!

His words take us right to the very heart of this part of his role, this specific link in the Service chain. I am coming to appreciate it is a chain that is anything but linear in fashion. It might have an obvious starting point; however from there it becomes an entwined and integrated *something*. I don't know how I would draw it, what shape I would use, or how I would represent the energy that pulses through it. Maybe by the end of our time together I will have a better idea. Maybe it doesn't matter. Surely, though, everything has a shape?

I put these thoughts from my mind and realise that I am tapping my pen against the words I have just written. I'm not doing it to make him glance – although he does – I'm just excited by what he might say next.

'You've made it clear to me Diego that Service is determined by the attitude and qualities of the staff, but I think there is a crucial ingredient that needs to be in place before that.'

'Which is?'

'You. The leader, the trainer, the role model. The person with the Service vision and the skills to turn it into a reality. You just said that your aim is to make your staff think like you. So you, the visionary, have to be in place to chart the direction for others to follow. You have to know exactly what great Service looks like and sounds like so that you can teach others to create it. You have to be here first, don't you?'

He nods. 'Of course, everything needs someone to go first. There always has to be that person with what you call a vision. Here...' his right hand waves gently at our surroundings, '...at The Waterside Inn, Mr Roux was that person.'

I ease back in my chair. I know the history of the British gastronomic revolution led by Michel Roux Snr. and his elder brother, Albert. So, as Diego talks, I note,

> It's interesting, but not surprising, that he's talking about his boss as the visionary before he'll start talking about himself. He's such an obvious and influential leader in his own right and yet he's always quick to assert Mr Roux's ultimate leadership. Another point, I think, to ask about later.

For the next few minutes Diego reminds me of how, in 1967, the two Roux brothers opened their restaurant, Le Gavroche, in Chelsea, London. Under their joint leadership, Le Gavroche went on to become the first British restaurant to gain three Michelin stars. In 1972, with several other successful restaurants under their banner, the brothers bought a traditional English pub in the quiet Berkshire village of Bray. The pub was transformed and The Waterside Inn was created. By 1974 the first Michelin star was achieved and the second followed in 1977. It took a further eight years of hard, consistent work before the much-coveted third star was awarded. One year later the brothers separated their business interests and Michel became the sole owner of The Waterside Inn. A year later Diego joined him.

I ask, wanting to bring the conversation back full circle, 'Why did Mr Roux invite you to work with him here?'

'Because he wanted to create the very best Service.'

'And?'

'The first thing I had to do, obviously, was assess the place. Mr Roux gave me permission to create the changes I wanted, which were based on my beliefs about Service and what guests need to experience in a restaurant.'

'Did the staff accept your philosophy and approach?'

'No, not everyone. It was quite difficult. The first thing you do when you are changing the culture is you look at your team. You speak to them if you need to, once, twice. If you see that things don't really change, then you change your staff. It's not easy. You have to make hard decisions. So that's what I did. It took me about six months. I changed about 40 per cent of the team. The most important thing to realise is that you cannot provide great Service by yourself. You have to have at least one or two people in the team who think like you. It's not just that they work like you – anyone can be trained to do that – they must believe in the same things. So I offered some people I knew a job and they followed me here. I believe in teamwork. You have to have the right people.'

'So, at the very beginning, it was essential to have some individuals working with you who already shared your philosophy and goals?

'Yes. They were my lieutenants. They understood me because they believed in the same things and they thought in the same ways as me.'

'So, coming back to the present day, how exactly do you get all staff to think like this, to think like you?

Back to the essential question, to the answer I was so keen to hear. During my years of observing Diego and his team I have seen very clearly how his staff seek to copy him, how he offers himself as a deliberate and powerful role model. I was intrigued to know how he influenced their mental processes rather than just their physical actions.

'When staff first come here they are all different, from different countries and backgrounds, with different languages, so first I get to know them and understand them. Then, very gently, I begin to work with them. I must gain their trust. When they can see that I trust them, even if it is only with small things, I begin to talk to them about my past. I let them see that I am like them, that I came from a very humble background, that I had to work hard and face challenges. Then they think, "He is just like me!" Then, bit by bit, I can encourage them to think like me. It is because I have gained their trust. They trust that I am not just there to make them work, to make them run, to simply pay them at the end of the month. They trust that there is more to it than that. And as their trust in me grows, so they think like me even more. Later, if they move on, if they go abroad to work, people report back to me, "They are just like you, Mr Diego!" They don't even realise they are doing it of course. It is just that, once you have someone's trust, your example becomes contagious. It becomes very contagious.'

He's talking to me again about the relationship between being the leader, the role model and the trainer. He has created here – and continually recreates – a Service-based culture that emanates from, and revolves around, his own example. I am sure that Diego has never studied the topic of *Influence*, academically at least, and yet he displays an intuitive understanding of just how to create it. He doesn't even wait until staff begin working with him; he starts influencing during the recruitment process.

I make the briefest note,

Everything is so joined up!

This is more a personal reminder that, during my time here, I need to keep looking out for and identifying the procedural congruency that is the corporate manifestation of his personal congruency. Service might well mean pleasing and never having to ask, but I'm getting the very clear sense that it also means an avoidance of gaps. Suddenly, I'm finding it easy to think that the poor Service I've experienced so often and in so many places was the result of gaps within the organisations.

Later, when I am alone, I write,

It's the gaps the customers fall through that costs businesses dearly. You can't provide great Service – and certainly not consistently (you might get lucky once in a while) – if there are gaps.

For example, Service staff should not have a gap between the smile on their face and the feeling in their heart. Their understanding of their product should be complete, no knowledge gaps. The procedures they are required to follow should simply and effectively support and enhance Service interactions, no gaps between organisational processes and customer-facing experiences. There should be no internal or external communication gaps; you have to deliver what you promise to (so be careful what you write on your website) and, when necessary, you must share information about customers in a timely and clear manner.

Reputations and return on investment disappear down these gaps. On one level organisations know this and yet so many still seek to close their Service gaps and measure how well they provide customer satisfaction through regimented form filling! What a great way to create another gap – between what the forms report and what your Service staff and their customers actually experience together.

Gaps, you can only avoid them if everything is joined up. Yet we can't create perfection, can we? A question for another day.

Now, though, my thoughts return to what Diego has just said, to his innate ability, to the ease with which he operates as the great Influencer. I can't help but measure him against available academic criteria.

Research[4] tells us that there are specific principles we can apply that increase our ability to influence others. These are:

~ Authority
~ Reciprocity
~ Likeness
~ Commitment and Consistency
~ Social Proof
~ Scarcity

Diego uses them all. His authority stems from his reputation as much as it does from his role. As human beings we are, it seems, more easily influenced by someone we acknowledge as an authority on their subject and/or by someone whose role gives them authority. Diego has both. His role and his level of expertise are indivisible. No gaps. It's one of the reasons why front-of-house personnel travel from all over the world to be trained and mentored by him.

Diego understands this. He wears his authority as comfortably as he does a suit. He uses it with ease and precision. He reveals it in varying degrees of light and shade according to his purpose and the needs of others. Whilst some might seek authority as an end in its own right, for him it is a natural and necessary foundation from which he

---

4 If you want to explore this further begin with the work of Robert Cialdini, Regents' Professor Emeritus of Psychology and Marketing at Arizona State University

can provide Service and business success, managing what he refers to as 'the difficult chain', the relationship between Service, quality, and profit. From the many hundreds of hours I have spent observing Diego at work, I have come to realise that he doesn't so much *use* authority as *share* it. And his authority is replenished through its sharing.

This sharing and serving sometimes creates more than a sense of gratitude in the recipient, it creates a powerful feeling of obligation. Reciprocity, the feeling of owing a debt, is a powerful influencer and motivator. Interestingly, experiments reveal that not only are many people compelled to repay a debt, they often do so by giving back more than they initially received. Diego has known this from an early age. The story of his time as a teenager working in a five star hotel in La Baule, demonstrates how quickly he learnt the value of giving – and going – first. For many years he has applied the power of reciprocity in his role as a trainer and mentor.[5] He gives because it is in his nature to do so and because he knows that it brings a range of rewards in its wake. He also knows that his authority adds power to the perceived value of his giving and, by extension, to the increased likelihood of significant reciprocity.

That likelihood is increased if we like the person we are engaging with. Diego *is* liked. Not only by his customers, but, even more impressively, by the staff he critiques, criticises,

5 He also recognizes the power of reciprocity in all his other interactions, including serving guests.

The Diego Masciaga Way

challenges and supports. Frédéric Poulette, the assistant Maître d'hotel says, 'People here respect Mr Diego so much. You don't want to disappoint him, to feel that you have let him down.'

It is important to remember that Diego recruits *for* likeness, employing those who already demonstrate at least some of his beliefs and attitudes and who demonstrate their desire to develop them further. He has a global reputation for excellence and an international network. It is known that he helps his staff to progress their careers. So it is hardly surprising staff both like him and want to be like him. The commitment to maintain the standards of Service that Diego demands, to avoid letting him and the guests down, is also developed little by little, day by day. As training progresses individuals come to understand and accept the Service-focussed, attention-to-detail, every-time-as-if-for-the-first-time, we-can-always-improve, culture that creates the remarkable levels of consistency for which The Waterside Inn is famous.

When Diego trains staff, whether formally or informally, he is acutely aware that he is developing individual buy-in to the organisational culture, as well as developing individual and team skills. He also deliberately and consistently repeats and reinforces his key messages about what Service is, how it should be delivered, and the outputs it should create.

I find myself fascinated by the fact that Diego creates within his team a consistent approach to what is, according to his own beliefs and practice, a bespoke activity. The more time I spend with him, the more I inevitably experience the compelling nature of his Service-related culture, at the heart of which are the two apparently simple beliefs:

Service begins and ends with a genuine smile

And

Every guest is unique and they should be treated as such

The consistency he develops is not a script-based approach in which the same phrases are learnt and repeated to all guests; or, indeed, in which the same behaviours occur in precisely the same way. Rather, it is a consistency underpinned by clearly expressed and shared beliefs, built around specific operational principles, and brought to life by the level of skill of individual staff and the overall cohesion of the team.

I am back, I realise, to the avoidance of gaps and to an increased understanding of just why training at The Waterside Inn is a continual, never-ending process. After all, if you base your Service on a rigidly adhered to formula that incorporates step-by-step behaviours, you don't need to develop the skills necessary to manage a bespoke service. The formulaic approach implies that customers can, at best, be pigeon-holed into certain categories and that each category can then be managed through the application of a specific procedure. For some – for too many, I fear – that's where Service starts and ends. For Diego, it's neither the start point nor the end point. For him, it has nothing to do with Service. Pure and simple.

And I do find a certain type of purity in Diego's understanding, pursuit and delivery of Service, something noble in his life-long commitment to it. There's nothing simple about it however. It stops being simple once you make Service bespoke and then deliver it in such a way that it doesn't create organisational chaos. At The Waterside Inn everything is bespoke. Yet the business structures and systems, the principles that Diego has established, have enough flexion to accommodate variation, and staff have the necessary skills to ensure they meet the personal needs of guests whilst maintaining cohesion.

If Diego's team were performers in a different domain – musicians or actors for example – they would be experts of improvisation rather than being dependent on a score or script. More challenging still, their form of improvisation is with their guests and not fellow professionals. That's why the continual training is needed, why only an organisation with Service at the very heart of its culture will ever commit to such a rigorous process. This culture, the accepted social proof, the agreed ways of behaving and *thinking*, combines with the final principle of influence – scarcity. This is reflected both in the unique nature of The Waterside Inn and in the example and teaching of Diego, to ensure an irresistible mix. It's no wonder professionals want to come and work here. It's no surprise that, despite Diego's willingness to train and support all of his staff, it is still too demanding for some.

I note,

The staff who come here and stay, who can cope with the demands and expectations of Diego, have no choice but to become really, really good. The training is non-stop, but, importantly, it is wrapped in a culture that has Service at its very heart and is intolerant of people who will not commit.

It's all-too easy to make comparisons between what is happening here and the approaches that underpin the training and development of elite military units. These include the inescapable culture with its unquestioned hierarchy, the sense of team above self, the absolute acceptance that excellence means getting all the little details right repeatedly and in being able to adapt appropriately under pressure, the never-ending rigour, the desire to be the very best, the all-encompassing sense that you are serving something greater than yourself.

It would be interesting and revealing to ask others throughout the Hospitality and Catering industry and, indeed, in other industries, the question, 'What great belief, principle or purpose do you serve through your work?'

If a clear, heart-felt answer is forthcoming one could then start exploring and measuring how precisely, successfully and consistently this was being achieved.

If such an answer is not forthcoming, it would perhaps be time for a different sort of conversation.

Back, though, to Diego. He is making a significant point about training that is often missed. It is this: the example set by the trainer, their ability to influence, demonstrate and inspire, is at least as important as the content they deliver.

The other realisation I'm addressing is that in many organisations staff training is either given by a separate, internal department or by external specialists; rarely by the team leader. Not here. Not with Diego in charge of Service. It's why I'm having difficulty writing about Diego the trainer, the mentor and the leader in linear fashion, because he is all three rolled up into one. And the benefits to him and his team (and, of course, their guests) are significant.

Given this, it is all too easy to imagine people from other businesses within and beyond the industry, saying, 'It's all well and good for him to take this hands-on approach and create bespoke Service, it's just not possible for us because our organisation is too big, or we are rarely ever face-to-face with our customers!'

I wonder how he would respond. One easy way to find out...

'Diego, do you really think that your approach to Service and staff training can be applied successfully in other businesses, to those with more staff, for example, or different ways of interacting with customers?'

His answer is instantaneous. 'Yes, I do. I think that if you can train forty people you can train two hundred. By which I mean you can train as many as you have. First of all you train three or four or five of your key staff. You train them to think like you and behave in your way. This is more important than just training them in the essential skills. So you focus on this. When they really think like you and they show it through their actions then these people will share this way of thinking and behaving with others. So it spreads to everyone.'

He pauses. I wait. His silent introspection is swift and then he clarifies, 'Although I say that I want my staff to think like me, it is very important that they keep and demonstrate their own personality and behave naturally. Sometimes people deliberately try to copy me. This is not necessary and it is not good. We can think in the same way and work to achieve the same things for our guests, we can follow the same principles and stay within the same guidelines and still be ourselves. We all have different personalities and different ways of showing and doing the same things. We must keep this. Real people must provide real Service. Guests need and deserve this.'

Diego nods. He smiles. I find it easy to imagine that a film of his real people providing real Service is playing in his mind. I also imagine that rather than just enjoying it, he is inevitably analysing it as if from a distance, observing the movement, the interactions, the pace and atmosphere, just as he does throughout every Service. I wonder if there is a specific film he returns to or if it is continually updated. I suspect the latter.

It's time to ask the next question, about the guidelines he has just referred to.

'Diego, beyond the skills your staff need to function well in a restaurant, what are the principles you base your Service training on?'

One hour later I have summarised the 10 principles that underpin Service the Diego Masciaga way. They are congruent and developmental.

1) 'Service begins with a genuine, heart-felt smile.'

2) 'Staff must always remember that every guest is different and that *everyone* is a guest – a person who just asks for a brochure and one who asks for the menu. Both deserve excellent Service.'

3) 'Every member of staff is involved in customer Service.'

4) 'If you are good to people who are not paying today they will come one day to pay.'

5) 'Too much Service is as bad as not enough.'

6) 'It is vital to know when to start serving and when to stop.'

7) 'Great Service is underpinned by the staff's ability to read people's minds, quickly and continually.'

8) 'Some people like to ask for Service; some just like to receive it. Staff have to recognise these differences and react accordingly.'

9) 'The guest is our guest until they leave, not until they pay.'

10) 'The ending of the Service is very, very important.'

It is interesting to note that whilst Diego shared and explained these principles not once did he feel obliged to make reference to technical skills such as carving, or clearing a table or managing a cheese trolley. I had asked him to ignore these elements of course, but he did so with such ease that it was clear he regarded the principles to be of greater significance. His response when I asked him about that was simple and to the point.

'Technical skills in any profession are obviously very important and they do play their part in creating Service. First, though, staff have to understand what Service is. Technical ability without this understanding will not ensure a great experience for the guest.'

'Are technical skills easier to learn than this understanding of the purpose and nature of Service?'

'They can be for some people. The truth is that even when teaching a skill, we can also be teaching, or reminding, staff of the other, *bigger* things. This is important to remember when providing training.'

It is also true that the 'bigger things' imply a mass of detail within their apparent simplicity. For example, the starting point that everyone you communicate with is a potential customer reinforces the point that Service is a

24/7 commitment. It requires staff to be *switched on*, to be identifying and satisfying individual needs, every time they communicate. The ability to recognise just how much Service different people want and ensuring that they get this delivered in the way that appeals to them best, reflects what Diego refers to as the need for staff to be able to 'read the minds' of guests; not only must this be done continually, it also needs to be done swiftly and the insights gained acted upon immediately.

His final principle, for all sorts of obvious reasons, is his emphasis on the value and importance of endings. Diego knows that a great experience is absolutely dependent on a great ending. It is the last thing that people remember, the part it is easiest to take away with you, the part that bridges the gap between experience and memory. The ending has to be at least worthy of everything that has gone before. If it isn't you are in trouble. If your aim is to start brilliantly and maintain excellence throughout, creating a standout ending is an obvious challenge. It is just one more demand that Diego places on his staff and that his training has to address.

Then, as if he really is reading my mind, he says, 'You have to understand your Service staff before you even think about understanding your guests. You have to get into the shoes of your individual staff, just as you do your guests.'

That, of course, is the difference between the leader and the team. He has to manage and influence his staff as carefully and accurately as he does his guests.

I write,

Service is Influence!

And then I add,

Service: congruency and contagion...

It's not, I realise, the best public strapline. I can't see too many people being attracted by the notion of contagion, but it summarises my current thinking. Great Service not only needs to be joined up, it needs to be based on a clear and accurate understanding of an individual guest's needs and the ability to then influence them positively. If it lacks that level of congruency, Service will lack consistency and it won't spread. If it doesn't spread it doesn't create the atmosphere in which guests can have the best possible time.

Congruency and contagion: I think it's accurate. It just needs to be reframed for marketing purposes. It is time now to enquire about the final two parts of the training mix.

'Diego, how do you use rewards to motivate staff and what sort of team-building activities do you do?

'Rewards are definitely important. I think that these little incentives are particularly useful when they are given unexpectedly. Incentives can be many different things. They can be extra time off. Or help with their family. It could be helping them to open a bank account, or just taking them home at the end of the evening. One of my boys did very well recently so I sent him to the Dorchester to eat there.'

I have noticed that when a member of staff demonstrates an interest in or aptitude for one particular aspect of service, Diego is quick to help them develop it further. Additional training is a reward not a duty, and it is clearly recognised as such by those who receive it.

The other aspect of staff development that is, in my experience, unique to the catering and hospitality industry, is the way individuals are encouraged and assisted to move on when they are ready for a new role in a different organisation. Diego makes full use of his extensive global network to help place his staff on their next step up the professional ladder. When the time is right he is keen to help them move on, confident in the remaining team and the success of his recruitment programme to maintain standards.

'As for team building,' Diego says with a slight smile, 'We do boat trips and sometimes we do paintball with the guns. They sting, but I have to go as well. I have to go because if I don't my team will ask why I am not there. Also, we will occasionally get together for a social event.'

I am really surprised that there are no more specific activities. When I question this further Diego explains that he believes the actual act of Service creates the necessary communication, understanding and trust upon which great teams are built. On that, our time together ends and I take my leave to write up my summary notes. Paintball with guns, I think to myself as I drive away from The Waterside Inn. And I have just made the argument that there is much in common here with the elite military!

Summary

There is, of course, much in common here with *all* elite environments. The common themes that are so easy to talk about and so nearly impossible to implement, manage and maintain are all present.

The lessons are:

Lesson no. 1

Elitism and excellence starts with recruitment. You have to know precisely what attributes you need if you are to maintain the highest of standards within your organisation. Accept no compromises throughout the selection process. Ensure that the people who do the recruiting know precisely what they are looking for and how to recognise it. Give them the freedom to be thorough and creative in how they do this.

Lesson no. 2

Attitude is key. Technique is teachable. Look for hunger, humility and honesty in the Service professionals you employ.

Lesson no. 3

Service is the glue that bonds the customer to the organisation. Service is influence. All staff are involved in Service. The only way to create and sustain elite levels of Service is to very deliberately establish and operate within a Service-based culture. This needs to be managed, measured and maintained by senior staff, the 'lieutenants' – the guardians of, and thought-leaders within, the organisation.

Lesson no. 4

It is the gaps the customers fall through that costs businesses dearly. You can't provide great Service consistently if there are gaps. Join everything up by focussing on the 3 Cs:

Cohesion, Consistency, Congruency

Lesson no. 5

Train staff to think like your thought leaders, to think in ways that support the culture. Training can be formal and informal. It must be continuous. Even when teaching technique, reinforce the essential principles and levels of understanding that underpin the culture and the expected standards. The example set by, and the abilities of, the trainer is at least as important as their knowledge. Trainers need to really understand the people they are training.

Lesson no. 6

Determine the level of teamwork you need and the extent to which daily organisational activities actually create that level. Only provide additional teambuilding activities if they do not. Provide bespoke, sometimes unexpected, rewards to thank and motivate staff.

∼

3

∾

LEADERSHIP

The first and last responsibility

∾

'The first responsibility of a leader is to define reality.
The last is to say thank you.'
Max de Pree

Stories and serving

The vast majority of Diego Masciaga's adult life has been spent closing the gap between the first and last responsibility of leadership. Just as customers fall through the gaps that organisations leave unfilled, so staff fall through the gaps that leaders leave unfilled. Whenever that happens, quality, cohesion and consistency fall away also. And whenever that happens, entire businesses can begin to slide.

Diego has such a clear vision of Service reality that his definition is absolute; there is no space for slippage. It combines an all-encompassing big picture with exceptional attention to detail. It is as complete as any great work of art. The only difference is that Diego's definition of Service reality, unlike art, is a living, breathing, 24/7, interactive experience that is ultimately entirely dependent on the quality of the interactions between staff and guests. Diego's reality is not only never-ending it starts afresh every day. It is a blank canvas framed by the Service principles that shape his world.

Diego, like all great leaders in business, knows that his definition of reality not only needs to be accepted by both staff and customers, it also needs to be highly valued by both. It needs to be real and aspirational. It must be consistently recognisable and yet always adapting to meet current needs. Perhaps most importantly, it needs to be *lived* and not simply talked about. It needs to be a reality rather than an undelivered promise forever trapped within the confines of a website, or a strategic vision written and repeated but never enacted.

Diego defines and shares his version of reality through the creation and sharing of compelling stories. He shares these stories, which are at the very core of his Service-based culture, through what he says and through what he does. He understands fully the power of storytelling. He has demonstrated this to me repeatedly throughout our many hours of conversations.

'Sometimes as the leader,' he says, 'you have to give direct, very clear instructions. This is especially true if you have little time available to you – in the middle of Service, for example. Sometimes you have the time and the opportunity to give an instruction by telling a story to your staff. When you do this they will not only be more entertained they will remember it better. The story must be true and it must have a good lesson inside it. It might be a lesson about how to behave in a certain situation or it might be a reminder of why Service is so important.

In our pre-service briefings, for example, I will talk about work, about guests, but I also tell stories about my experiences and about how I want them to behave both at work and outside. It's very important that staff realise they are representing the brand even when they are not at work. I have to know what staff do and about their lifestyle. I cannot afford them mixing with the wrong people. Stories are a good way to reinforce this. Remember, the basis of restaurant Service, the techniques, never change. Beyond that you have to tell stories to keep your staff motivated and entertained when they are learning. These stories also, of course, remind them that you are the leader because you are the one telling the stories.

The other stories that are also important are the ones that other people say about you. People like the critics and journalists, and those who give you awards. Of course, we cannot hope for them to say great things if we are not doing great things. So everything we do here comes first. As I have said the stories have to be true and they can only be true if we are truly providing great Service.'

It also needs to be borne in mind that, as his team is

international, Diego is telling stories that are understood by and motivate people from different cultures. His success at doing so reflects far more than the fact that he can speak several languages. It is due rather to his instinctive ability to create stories with structure and content that our minds naturally search for. Essentially his stories always have a clear setting and sense of time, they centre upon a problem, a challenge, a need that has to be met, they progress in obvious, easy to follow steps and they always provide the resolution.

The great American writer and humourist Samuel Langhorne Clemens[6] once wrote, 'I like a good story well told. That is the reason I am sometimes forced to tell them myself.' Diego bases his well-told, good stories, on any mixture of his experiences, skills, memories, beliefs, principles and goals. He knows that the nature and quality of the reality his staff and guests experience at any one time is determined by the extent to which his stories have been heard and absorbed by those who regard him as their leader.

He uses his stories to develop and reinforce those attitudes he prizes most amongst his staff. Through the use of stories he teaches others to think like him. He is fully aware that, as the role model, he is a performer as well as simply a narrator. He understands that through his actions he is not only sharing or reinforcing a story, he is also encouraging those who have watched him in action to tell others, to become storytellers

6 Better known as Mark Twain.

on his behalf. The importance of 'spread' is demonstrated once again.

Diego also shares stories with guests. These are only ever based on what the guests want to talk about. Their purpose is engagement, to develop that important sense of likeness, to create feelings of comfort, to help develop the atmosphere he wants within the restaurant. Diego shares stories with guests as easily and, apparently, effortlessly as he does with staff.

I note,

> And his staff have no option but to see and hear him at work... Stories told and encouraged, demonstrations, conversations, formal and informal training...If Service is 24/7 so is leadership. If Service is Influence so is leadership. But how do you successfully and congruently combine the two? How do you lead and serve your staff without confusing them about the nature of your relationship? Or without confusing yourself about just who you are and the purpose of your role?

'Diego would you agree that, on one level, your role requires you to serve your staff as well as serving your guests?'

'Yes, absolutely. But it is a complicated thing. It is very important that my staff know that I am here for them, to support them and look after them. All staff have to feel happy and secure before guests can feel the same. Only happy staff can provide great Service time after time. So I can only have positive people here. This means that if a member of staff complains and moans and I cannot stop them, then I have to tell them to go. Negativity spreads. It can damage the atmosphere within the team and the quality of the Service we provide. I cannot afford that. Fortunately that type of thing does not happen very often, but it is another reason why I have to know all of my staff as individuals. I have to understand them very well, in the same way that I have to understand my guests. Only when you know your staff individually can you really know how to make them happy, how to reward and train them, even how to tell them off in a way that will make them feel good eventually. As the leader you have to listen to all your staff equally and make them feel good. The kitchen porter needs to feel as important and valued as the maître'd. It is a fact that in our industry guests rarely praise cleaners and porters, for example. However they will often praise front-of-house staff. I have to compensate for this. Some staff do work that is only noticed when it is not done or done badly. They are the *backstage* people and they must be praised equally.'

'Given that you are combining these two different roles, how do you manage to serve and lead at the same time?'

'Ah, well, that is an interesting thing. First of all, staff have to know that you are the boss. The only way they can truly show you this is by giving you their trust. But you have to earn that trust in the first place! I will explain how I do that in a moment. To answer your question, though, once I have the trust of my team and I can see that they know I am the boss, then I can really serve them. You see, at the end of the day we are all human beings. I look at my team and of course they remind me of myself thirty years ago. I see myself in them. Only thirty years ago I didn't have anyone to mentor me. So I try to give my staff what I never had, just like a parent does for their own children. I make sure that they also know that if I tell them off it is for their own good, as part of their learning and development, not because I need to satisfy feelings of anger. In fact, I often say to them, "The day when you need to start worrying is when Mr Diego stops talking to you, stops advising you or even stops telling you off, because when I do any of those things – even telling you off – it is because I believe in you and I want to improve you."

One other thing is that if a member of staff from another restaurant comes to eat at the Waterside Inn I treat them like kings and queens, because I want my staff to be treated like this when they visit other restaurants, and also because I want to share my respect for our profession. In doing this I also get respect back from the profession.'

Diego stops talking and sips politely at his coffee whilst I write,

He provides bespoke leadership as well as bespoke training and bespoke Service! Everything, from recruitment onwards, has been based on an in-depth understanding of others.

And reciprocity is there again! He knows that if he shows his genuine respect for others he is most likely to get it back, whilst also promoting The Waterside Inn and its reputation for providing the very best Service.

The need for the leader to gain the trust of his or her staff is something to ask more about and what a brilliant way to frame a telling off, as a positive sign of care and belief in potential. The great double bind in this is that staff will actually prefer a telling off to being ignored!

Running through it all is a very powerful sense of humanity. What was it he said near the start of his answer, "At the end of the day we are all human beings." I think my previous list of 3 H's has just been developed by a factor of one.

When I stop writing Diego stops drinking. Thankfully, I know precisely what my next question is. 'How do you gain the trust of your team?'

Now it's my turn to watch Diego's mind at work. I get the sense that his answer is going to be multi-layered, that he is not searching to identify the parts but rather ensuring that he has them in the right order before he speaks. The silence stretches slightly. His eyes flicker from side to side. He looks like a man ensconced within his own mental library, scanning the shelves. I prepare myself for when he comes out. Then he looks at me, draws a slight breath and we are off.

'First, it starts with you as the leader. It starts with the example you set, particularly the example you set when you are under pressure. You see if you are a leader, no matter how much pressure you face, you always have to be in control.

If the team see the boss lose control everything crumbles. It's the end of it. So, if you are the leader, never show you are stressed, never show your anger, never show that you are tired. You always have to be 100 per cent. Every morning when I arrive here I must be 100 per cent even if there is a problem, even if I didn't sleep last night.'

Diego pauses. I glance up from my note making. I had presumed that he was just giving me time to write. Only he isn't. He is using the silence to emphasise his point, to make sure that I feel the full weight of what he has just said.

You always have to be 100 per cent.

Really? How many people actually go to work believing only 100 per cent will do? That if they only give 99 per cent they will have failed? More to the point, how many leaders do this?

What is more interesting is that Diego doesn't believe in human perfection in the workplace. He doesn't think that people can create perfect Service any more than they can produce a perfect product. So, for him, 100 per cent does not mean perfection it just means everything you've got. If you keep working hard and training and learning your 100 per cent next year will be better than your 100 per cent this year. It is the leader's responsibility to motivate staff into wanting to give 100 per cent and to want to keep improving upon it. It is the leader's wisdom to know that sometimes staff will fall short precisely because we are human beings.

From himself, though, Diego expects nothing less than his very best. It is one of the most important ways in which he serves his team. He is striving always to be the exemplary role model.

When he sees that I have finished my consideration, Diego continues. 'Also, whenever I see that a member of my team is struggling a little bit I go to them straight away. As the leader it is part of my job to lift them up. I find a way to make them feel better, to have more energy, to be comfortable again. For my staff Diego is the cushion.'

He beams. It is clearly a line that he likes.

'Leaders,' he concludes, 'need to remember that staff will follow their example. So if they see that you are always aiming higher, higher, higher, they will do the same. It is only natural.'

I can't help but smile at the almost childlike simplicity in what he has just said. After all, it is only natural or, perhaps, it would be more accurate to say, it is only possible, if you have recruited the right staff in the first place. If the leader is as irresistible as Diego. If the leader is the ideal role model who also knows how to create and define a reality that is at once desirable and challenging. Who is a great storyteller. Who always gives 100 per cent no matter what.

'Diego, as you have already said, we are all human beings. So how can you be 100 per cent at all times?'

I hear the question and recognise immediately that we are at one of the most important and potentially revealing moments of my study. We are at a crossroads. Sometimes you can plan a route towards a crossroads moment. Sometimes, like now, they happen spontaneously. I feel my heart rate speed up. How will he answer this?

He replies so quickly and with such a sudden shift in attitude and demeanour that I find myself once again moved by his honesty and the level of commitment to Service it implies.

'How can I be 100 per cent at all times?' He repeats. 'Willpower.' He tips his head; someone else might have winked at me instead. 'And great acting.'

We both laugh. It is the laughter people share when the truth undoes the hope within the question. There is no great secret, no magic formula or potion for achieving and maintaining excellence. You just have to want it so much – *care* so much – that even when you don't feel at your best you fake it so well nobody notices. At the end of the day there is just a man inside the Batman suit. It is when we remember that we feel the greatest admiration for what he achieves and for the sacrifices he makes.

What was it Diego said at the very beginning of our time together? He said, *'It isn't a job, it's a life.'* I'm getting it. If you can't say that with your hand on your heart you have no chance of achieving and maintaining excellence. If you are lucky, you just might be great for a few days.

The bottom line is there is absolutely nothing natural about excellence. In fact, the opposite is true. Excellence is about as unnatural as you can get. Imitation, however, is far more common. Diego is right that staff will be influenced by their leader's example.

I note,

Follow my leader – it's more than just child's play.

As ever Diego makes no attempt to read my notes or to ask about them. I'm guessing that before we began this process together he had made the decision to trust me. He's good at trust, both earning it and giving it. I suspect that in his world-view, trust is the highest currency. That is why I need to know more. This time he doesn't wait for me to speak again. The agenda has already been set and he is keen to talk.

Trust, loneliness, balance and boundaries

'As I have mentioned before, leadership for me is about trust.' He says, turning to face me more fully than he usually does. 'The leader has to know how to gain the trust of their team and how to show that they, in turn, trust their team back. You see, you are not a leader if people don't follow you and they won't follow you if they don't trust and respect you. I make it clear to all of my staff that they are vital; without them I am nothing. Leaders cannot exist on their own. You cannot be the leader, the boss, unless you have people who are willing to accept you in that position. Of course, I am the person who sets the rules, who has the responsibility for telling people what to do and how to do it, but in our profession there is always a need for someone to do that. To do it well, though, the leader has to build good relationships. I see everyone in my team as an individual and I talk to them as individuals. I speak at their level. When you speak at their level, over time they come to trust and count on you, almost like a friend or a father, within boundaries of course. Then I can ask them to take the extra step and they will do it with pleasure. What is also important is that when I speak to them I let them get to know more about me. I want them to understand that when I was their age I went through everything they are experiencing here. I was just like them. It is extremely important that they know my history, where I have come from and what I have been through, so that they know I understand how they are feeling and they also know that they can achieve as I have.'

I resist the temptation to write even more notes about how he so deliberately uses likeness to influence others. I can't help but reflect, however, how well he creates a sense of commitment within his team to him, as their leader. Whilst everyone he employs has to commit to the cause of Service, Diego is clearly aware that every cause needs a figurehead. He is it. The individuals within his team work for The Waterside Inn and have their own professional goals and aspirations, yet Diego is their immediate role model, their trainer and mentor, their supporter and critic, their inspiration. Leaders not only need to be acknowledged by others, they need others to commit to them. Diego makes it easy for his staff to commit to him. His leadership style creates more than trust. It creates loyalty.

'I will do anything for them,' Diego says. 'As the leader, I will do everything in my power to help them learn and then progress in our profession. Also I have to be honest and consistent. If you tell someone, for example, that you will promote them and you don't then people very quickly stop trusting you. As a leader and a teacher, I need to be very patient; day after day I am repeating instructions, requests, to my staff. If I need to tell someone off, I will do it, but I will never emotionally blame them. I will never crush an individual's emotions. If you take away someone's confidence you can crush them. I know that feeling and I will never do that to anyone in my team.'

Diego has never forgotten the challenges he faced as a young adult making his way through his chosen profession. He genuinely empathises with those he employs and leads. He also understands fully the power of deliberately sharing messages such as 'I understand you because I went through what you are going through now' and 'I will always provide you with support and direction'. It's just one more example of how he manages to combine humanity and a desire to serve with his ability and authority as the leader.

'There are two more things I do that develop trust,' he says. 'The first thing is to protect them from complaints. Fortunately, we have very, very few complaints, but they do happen occasionally. Whatever the nature of the complaint, whether it is about food, Service, the rooms or the garden, I come first. I deal with it. I will not give my team the pressure of dealing with complaints. And I will never let a guest tell off a member of staff; I insist they talk to me. I believe that everything starts with management and leadership.

That is why I am never in my office all day. It is why I take responsibility for the quality of staff training. I think that, no matter what business you are in, the ability of the staff is a reflection of the ability of their managers. If someone is not good enough in their role, it is fair to ask questions of their leader not of that member of staff. Leaders protect their staff by helping them to be excellent at what they do, not just by managing complaints.

The second thing, as we discussed earlier, is that I show my team that I trust them. Leaders, I think, should always be looking for opportunities to demonstrate *their* trust in individuals and in the team as a whole. If you show that you trust someone, they are more likely to trust you in return. It is even more special when the leader shows that they trust you. Then you feel the need to live up to their trust and you feel grateful and proud in yourself because you know it means that you are good at your job. Let me give you an example. Recently we had a Michelin Inspector dining with us. I told one of the younger members of my team to carve the duck in front of the Inspector. He was very surprised that I chose him to do it, and he was a little scared because he knew it was a very important thing. Anyway, he did a good job as I knew he would and the Inspector was impressed. That day I won a new member of staff because he knew then that I trusted him.'

It isn't only training that Diego does little by little, day by day, I realise. It is also building trust. If the quality of Service bonds the guest to the organisation, it is trust that joins and holds the professional team together. I write so quickly it's barely legible:

> Service and Trust! They are so inter-connected I don't know how to separate them! Service – *pleasing* – is a trust-building activity. Given that, all businesses in every industry should define customers as:
>
> *Those people who put their trust in us.*
>
> If they did that they would have no choice but to create Service-based cultures.

Back here, at The Waterside Inn, I am also considering the fact that Diego, the leader and protector of his team, is a man alone. I think back to the stories he has told me of his trips to work in France whilst he was still nothing more than a boy, and his later move to work for Alain Chapel. It is becoming increasingly clear to me that he personifies the loneliness that inevitably accompanies great leadership. I ask the question without warning.

'Diego, do you enjoy being lonely?'

As he looks at me he becomes suddenly very still. I find myself wondering for the first time if I have asked something too personal. I match his stillness and wait.

'I like to be lonely sometimes,' he says finally. 'As a child I used to fish alone. I still do this occasionally as a way of relaxing. Just down there,' he gestures along the riverbank. 'I

The Diego Masciaga Way

don't go far away, but I go there sometimes just for an hour or two.' He nods. 'I think I have always found it easy to be comfortable when I am by myself. And because of the work that I do I need time every week when I can be silent and relax.'

'Rest is important?'

'Yes. It is one of the most important things.'

Despite his own incredible work rate, Diego encourages all of his staff to 'stick to their hours'. He believes that it is a mistake for leaders to expect everyone in their team to work the same hours as themselves.

'If, as an employee, you see your boss is always there one hour before you and is always staying one hour or more after you, it can be de-motivating. As an employee you feel that you can never catch up with your boss. This is a bad feeling. So I make clear to everyone if I come here early or stay late it is just something I do because my role requires it. No one else in the team is in my role, so they have to manage their time differently.'

I reflect briefly on his acute level of self-awareness. He knows he is the role model, so he is as clear with his staff about those aspects of his behaviour they *shouldn't* copy as he is those they should.

'Personally,' Diego continues, 'I think if you want a person to perform at his or her best, you have to get the right hours of work. Obviously, if you work for sixteen hours every day, for ten to twelve hours you will be productive. The other four you will be less so. We need to get the balance right.'

'And have you got the balance right?'

'I believe I have – as much as it is possible. Every week I am able to enjoy time at home with my family and that is very important. I can switch off. Some people cannot switch off at all and I have learnt to do that.'

'How? Who taught you?'

Diego's hands spread open. His head inclines briefly. It is the nearest I have seen him come to a shrug. 'I taught myself.'

'Is everything you learn now self-taught?'

'No. I still learn many things from our guests. And also I learn many things from my wife. I don't need to learn technique any more, but I need to follow the world as it changes. My wife and my daughters help me with this. I listen to them carefully. I am blessed to have such a wonderful, understanding family.'

I think to myself, the loneliness of the long-distance leader…I realise that Service and trust are meant to be together, but balance and loneliness? That sounds like a much more complicated fit. Perhaps only those people who are used to being on the edge really understand balance? The image of a tightrope walker balancing precariously above Niagara Falls slips into my mind. Making that crossing once successfully would be an amazing achievement. Diego has been up there for three decades. I note,

Longevity and consistency – another topic to address.

Then we move on. I want to ask him about his leadership style. I want to know if it is an instinctive reflection of his personality or more deliberately chosen.

'Diego, it is very clear that you operate through a hierarchical structure and that, as the leader, you are autocratic in style. You are clearly the boss who makes the decisions and directs operations. Why do you choose that style instead of a more democratic approach?'

'Again, there are several reasons. First of all Service in a restaurant is a time of great pressure. Everything has to be precise. Timings have to be exact. Success is dependent on teamwork. Everyone has a task, a designated task, but on their own they cannot achieve anything. It is a team effort, from the receptionist who takes the booking to the valet who parks your car when you arrive. After all, they are the first person you talk to and the first person you see. Throughout Service the restaurant staff have to rely on each other. They rely on someone else to serve the water, or the bread, or the food or wine. If they don't work together the final result is not there. Everyone knows we are here to work together. Someone has to be in charge of this. That is my responsibility. Staff have to follow instructions and they have to know their particular role. During Service there is no time for long conversations, or discussions or explanations. They have to be good at following directions without question. It is only later, sometimes a day or two after a particular Service, when we will talk in more detail if it is necessary to learn a lesson.

Because of the pressure the staff work under it is necessary, as I have already said, to provide rewards occasionally. After all, everyone likes it when the leader says "Thank you". There are so many ways I can do this. For example, I entered one member of the team into a competition. I told him that he needed to win it! And he did! He was so excited and grateful. He saw it as a reward because he knew that I wouldn't have entered him if I didn't think he was excellent. Sometimes we reward by paying for staff to have little holidays in other Relais and Chateaux establishments. Mr Roux is very generous in this way. Also, of course, sometimes a reward can be financial. Money, though, is not the only – or even the most important – reward. Other things like how we feel about ourselves, our sense of self-worth, our development, are also important. Being given a new responsibility is a reward. Being picked to serve prestigious guests is a reward.

During Service, though, staff are not thinking of such rewards. They are too focussed on pleasing our guests to think about themselves. That is the point of Service. *Pleasing*. We know that we achieve this and that the way we do it works. The leader has to lead. When you are working under pressure too many chiefs is worse than too many Indians.'

He smiles and I return it. He continues almost immediately.

'It is also comforting for the team to know that, at such times, they have a leader they can turn to if they are not sure, someone who will make the decision for them. Sometimes it is true that staff might not always like a leader who is clearly in charge. Sometimes, though, they are also very grateful to have that leader there. Even if the leader is being stern for a few seconds.' He smiles again. 'Of course, for this to work well the leader has to know exactly what he is doing.'

When I ask Frédéric Poulette about his leader's approach during Service he gives a wry grin, 'It is true, Mr Diego has two faces. He has the face with the customers – smiling, gentleness, everything. And then, you know, he can have another face...The great thing is that, even if you don't agree with him fully, at least 95 per cent of what he says is always right. And he always explains things in a way that you have to agree with. Mr Diego is always one step ahead. I try to be one step ahead of everyone else, but he is always ahead of me.'

I refer back to my notes about the similarities with the elite military. Whilst restaurant Service is clearly not a matter of life and death, it seems to me that in one sense Diego has created a culture in which people approach it almost as if it is. They recognise that every Service is a once-in-a-lifetime opportunity to get it right, that how brilliant they were yesterday is irrelevant, that high-level teamwork is essential, and that direct, obvious and unquestioned leadership is vital to success in time-pressured situations in which only the highest standards of performance and outcome are accepted.

I write,

Under pressure the explanations stop and direct orders are given. Diego can do this because he is always one step ahead of everyone else. That means he is far enough ahead to provide direction and yet close enough to be heard and understood.

One step ahead...A position of responsibility and reassurance.

Although The Waterside Inn operates through a hierarchical, role-bound, structure, Diego has, by his own admission, no limits when it comes to helping his staff. He uses the power of his role, his vast experience and his seemingly endless network, to support, develop and progress the careers of those in his team. It is another essential part of the taken-for-granted culture here. What impresses me particularly, though, is the fact that this is balanced by very clear role boundaries that are never challenged. And these role boundaries are as clear for Diego as they are for everyone else.

He has worked for the same boss, Michel Roux Snr., for over three decades, and yet there is still a very deliberate formality between the two. Diego says,

'With Mr Michel I always say Mr Roux. I've been with him for over 30 years, but I still call him Mr Roux (it is only Mrs Roux who I would call by her first name, Robyn, as this is the way she has always wanted to be addressed). That's one reason why our relationship has always been very good. I always think that in business or at work it is not right to become too friendly with your boss. If Mr Roux needs to tell me something, he can. It's no problem. If I need to fight back, to give my opinion, I can also. Our relationship is very, very strong.'

Despite being an authoritative leader in his own right, Diego also knows the importance of managing upwards. He shifts from playing the role of the boss to that of what he refers to as "no.2" with obvious ease. Not surprisingly, he is determined to serve his boss with the same skill and commitment that he does his staff and guests. And, not surprisingly, he brings the same mind reading skills to the task.

He explains it thus, 'You have to put your mind inside the brain of your boss; you have to know how it feels to be in their shoes. You also have to be happy being no.2.'

Throughout my time with Diego and during my consequent musings about Service and why it seems that so few people want to truly commit to providing it, I have returned repeatedly to the topic of ego and the attraction of power. By power I mean acknowledged and demonstrable authority, the power to control and command, the power that comes with certain highly valued roles, the power that is usually resource-rich, the power that is sought after by many. I can't help but think that desire for this type of power, coupled with a well-developed ego, inevitably prevents a deep understanding of the nature and purpose of Service and of the very different type of power that it represents.

Only recently I thanked an assistant in a shop by saying, 'That was absolutely brilliant Service. I really appreciate it.' It was clearly not what she wanted to hear. No sooner had she finished her abrupt reply than she turned her back and walked away. Before she left me she said, 'I don't serve! I hate it when people suggest that I do!'

Please understand I'm not sharing this as a criticism of the young woman. I fear her thoughts and feelings about

Service are common and therefore difficult to resist. I am certain, though, that they are mistaken. Diego's example makes it clear that even leaders – *especially* leaders – have a duty to serve others.

Diego serves his team by setting the vision, making the rules, developing their abilities and their careers, guiding them through Service and reprimanding when necessary. He is not part of the team. He is the leader. He makes the decisions. He has the final word. He has the power. It is not an equal relationship and they would not achieve excellence if it were. They all understand this and are happy with it.

Diego serves Michel Roux Snr. just as happily. He switches from being no.1 to being no.2 in a heartbeat. The man who is acknowledged as a world leader has his own boss. I'm not sure though that he has very much by way of an ego floating around. If he does, he has it so well under control that it is confined to the shadows.

My note reads,

Maybe when there are no gaps, when you have everything really well joined up, there is no space for ego?

It is certainly not because of ego that Diego insists on the use of titles. He does this to establish and maintain roles and role boundaries. To his staff he is always 'Mr Diego' just as, to him, Michel Roux Snr. is always 'Mr Roux'. In both cases the word "Mr" is used as an honorific, creating distance and respect. The title reflects and reminds all involved of the established hierarchy. When staff refer to 'Mr Diego' (or, indeed, when he refers to 'Mr Roux') there is a very clear sense that the person identified has experience, skill and insight that deserves to be acknowledged and valued. It reminds me of the Japanese use of the word *Sensei,* which is loosely translated as teacher but more accurately means *one who has gone before.* In the eyes of his staff Diego is certainly the one who has gone before. He makes that clear in the stories he tells. He demonstrates it through his expertise.

Interestingly, when staff refer to Diego the honorific is followed by his first name, thus combining authority and informality, distance and closeness, hierarchy and connection. It is another example of how an apparently simple cultural convention absorbs and then gives out far more meaning and influence than would seem apparent at first glance.

Diego does more than simply glance at the interplay within the hierarchy below him. He is acutely aware of the ambition amongst his team members and that there are limited internal opportunities for promotion. Satisfying an individual's desire for progression is a task he welcomes. It proves that he has, indeed, recruited those with the hunger to move up through the ranks.

'I stress to my team,' he tells me, 'never do a job if you are only there to warm up a chair.'

Diego recognises immediately whenever a member of staff is ready for the next level in the hierarchy. If he does not have that position available for them, he simply uses his network to help them to find it elsewhere.

Diego explains, 'My job as the leader is to study my staff and recognise and use their individual forte. I have to know how to make use of their strengths. When, for example, someone develops to a point at which they are ready for the role of no.2 in a great restaurant, I then have to help them to move on. I know that their strengths can no longer be developed with us because the no.2 role is filled here. So if that person stays with us for too long they will become disheartened and disinterested. That is not good for them and it is not good for us. Let me give you an example. I had a member of staff start here as a kitchen porter. Before that he had worked as a painter. After a while I moved him into house-keeping, then into wine and then other aspects of our work. Over time his knowledge and skills developed considerably. Eventually a position as assistant restaurant manager in Mr Roux's restaurant in Vietnam became available. He now has that role! Knowing who to recruit and how to develop them is vital. Knowing when it is time to let them go, so that they can gain new experiences elsewhere, is just as important.'

It is an approach to leadership and staff development that I have not encountered in other industries. In my experience most organisations are desperate to hold on to staff they have invested time and money in, especially when they think those members of staff are good at their job! Yet this more global view of staff development, this use of a network that staff are actively moved through, clearly plays its part in the creation and maintenance of excellence. It also promotes the standard of individual brands and the sharing of principles, philosophies and skills.

Diego knows that when he helps someone to move elsewhere, they will automatically be viewed as a former member of *his* team, as a representative of the standards of Service synonymous with The Waterside Inn. He isn't just helping an individual to develop; he is promoting the brand and showing his commitment to the industry as a whole. It is ethical and business-smart. It creates community within a competitive environment. It provides benefits to all, including guests. It is another reminder that Service creates a power all of its own.

I ask, 'Can everyone get to the top of the hierarchy? Can you train everyone to become no.1?'

'I don't think so. Some people naturally belong in certain roles. It is where they feel most comfortable. I have to help people reach the level and the role that is best for them. That is why I say that I need to understand their strengths. People must always do the best they can. Then they will eventually become the best they can be, even if that isn't the best there is.'

*The best there is...*Our meeting ends with the phrase still in my mind. I had always guessed that it would be lonely and uncomfortable on the mountaintop. After all, not many people get that high and the air is thin when you do. I wonder if it means you are too busy struggling to enjoy the view?

Diego never appears to be struggling. That's part of the deal. Actually it is a significant part of how he views his role and responsibility as a leader. He lives on the mountaintop. He makes it look easy. He helps those around him forge their own route.

I settle down to write my summary notes from a far more comfortable place. Base camp. Looking up.

Summary

Great Service is dependent upon great leadership. It can be argued that leadership is more a way of being, of thinking, acting and interacting, than it is a specific level in a hierarchy. Although it can be both. Leadership, like Service, is a 24/7 commitment. Essentially leaders have to successfully and continually answer the questions, 'Where are you leading us?' and 'Why are you the right person to do this?' Leaders have to answer these questions in ways that motivate their staff and gain their support, because leaders don't exist until other people give them permission to lead. Great leaders remember this.

The lessons are:

Lesson no. 1

Leadership *is* Service. Most obviously leaders serve their staff, their customers and their business. Leaders serve their staff by being the role model, providing formal and informal support, giving rewards, dealing with complaints and, if done well, giving necessary criticism. Leaders serve their staff best when they understand them as individuals.

Lesson no. 2

Leaders need to be accomplished and strategic storytellers. Stories play a vital role in defining reality. Stories need to be told well by a storyteller who is well regarded by the audience. The stories told need to be relevant to the audience and easily understood. Stories can be used to teach, motivate, inspire, reinforce important ideas, behaviours or ideals, create feelings of likeness or encourage change. Stories spread. Customers, critics, even competitors will tell stories about you; leaders and their teams need to do everything in their power to influence these.

Lesson no. 3

Leadership, Service and trust are interconnected. You cannot function successfully as a leader without the trust of those you lead. To earn trust leaders have to show trust. Trust can be developed through the acts of Service identified in Lesson no. 2 and storytelling. Customers – *guests* – can be defined as people who put their trust in the businesses with whom they engage. Businesses need to honour that trust through great Service.

Lesson no. 4

Leaders need to adapt their communication and leadership style to suit the situation. When the team is working under pressure with obvious time constraints, provide simple, direct and clear instructions; explanations can be shared at a later date. No matter what the task, leaders always need to be one step ahead, providing direction and reassurance.

Lesson no. 5

Loneliness is an inevitable part of leadership. Leaders are 'of' the team, not 'in' the team. Leaders have to know how and when to create boundaries that cannot be crossed and how and when to be boundary-free. As influential role models, leaders have to make clear to staff what aspects of their own behaviour should be disregarded. Leaders also often need to know how to manage upwards. Leaders stand alone in the space between their team and their own superior.

Lesson no. 6

Leaders must remember to say, 'Thank you.' Rewards are essential. Rewards need to demonstrate that the leader understands the individuals in their team. Rewards can take many forms; match the reward to the recipient.

∽

4

≈

DELIVERING
OUTSTANDING
SERVICE

What you make others see

≈

'Art is not what you see, but what you make others see.'
Edgar Degas

Simplicity, invisibility and mind reading

Diego Masciaga is an artist and an illusionist. He trains his team to be illusionists also. The illusion they create whilst providing world-class Service is that it is easy. They create this illusion by doing everything in their power to make their work invisible. Having watched them perform this illusion countless times, I know how it is achieved. I am going to share it with you.

It is based on misdirection and expertise. That makes it pretty much like every other great illusion, when you think about it. At The Waterside Inn guests are encouraged to look and think in certain ways and whilst that is happening the team of highly trained professionals applies skills that are so finely honed they are barely visible.

Only unlike every other great illusion the trick here is that the exceptional Service provided is *real*. It influences, shapes and enhances the experience of guests. It turns the present into unforgettable memories. The illusion that Diego and his team create is actually the illusion created by all who are the very best in their respective endeavours. It is the illusion that it is all so simple anyone could do it.

To recognize this as an illusion we first of all have to understand the nature of the simplicity on show. It is, as Oliver Wendell Holmes would describe, 'simplicity on the far side of complexity'. It is the simplicity that only the very best performers, the greatest of experts, can demonstrate. It is the simplicity that incorporates all that is needed and nothing more. It is the simplicity that reminds us that elegance is an extreme without extravagance.

'Too much Service is as bad as not enough,' Diego says.

It is 10am on an overcast November Monday. Diego begins our meeting by repeating this, one of his favourite mantras. It is the philosophical foundation for the invisibility and simplicity that is so highly prized.

'Service must be very discreet,' Diego continues, 'formal but at the same time informal. It must always be there but the guest must not see it. If a glass is nearly empty, staff should be aware and ready to act. If guests are talking, staff should leave them alone. We should always be looking and interpreting. Obviously nobody is perfect. If I was perfect I would be up there...' He gestures heavenward. '...But here we aim to get as close as we can.'

Whilst the guests are irresistibly encouraged to turn their attention elsewhere, into their own personal world, Diego's staff combine their individual expertise with exceptional teamwork and clear direction from their leader to repeatedly produce a performance that is meant to be so good that you miss it.

Diego has long known that excellence has three measures. Firstly that it looks easy to do. Secondly that it seems simple in construction and purpose. Thirdly that the outcomes it creates are exceptional.

'If a guest sees too much Service it is really bad,' Diego says again. 'Perfect Service is when you get what you need before you ask for it.'

And so he takes us back effortlessly to his inspiration, his mother, and the first lesson she ever taught him about Service.

'Whenever I needed something, she was always there ahead of me. She always seemed to know what I needed before I had to ask.'

He visits home, he tells me, once a year, in January when The Waterside Inn closes for its annual break. I find myself remembering the stories he told of himself as a young boy fishing alone. I think of him as a teenager in a grand French hotel by the coast, serving dogs because he wasn't regarded as skilled enough to serve their owners; yet being smart enough to know that he really was. I imagine him travelling back to his room in the early hours of a cold winter morning after yet another day organizing empty bottles in the restaurant of Alain Chapel.

I write,

He has committed his life to Service excellence based on that very first lesson he learnt from his Mother. He has paid his dues. He has done everything that was necessary to achieve the standard he sought. He has created it here, at The Waterside Inn, but where else does he find it? Possibly nowhere. That's the one gap he cannot fill – the level of Service he experiences elsewhere.

I just have to ask him.

'Diego, before we talk about how you provide such great Service here, I'd like to ask you what you think – how you feel – about the standards of Service you experience day-to-day?'

He sighs, considers briefly. He chooses his words carefully.

'The level of Service overall is very poor. This is my experience in many shops, banks, restaurants and hotels. Everywhere. Why is this? Well, we know that if you recruit the right people and train them and lead them well you can create something great. The problem is when the recruitment is not good and then when the people who lead – leaders

The Diego Masciaga Way

who are on the floor with their staff – are either not there or are not training, demonstrating, motivating, and reminding everyone of just how Service should be. If these leaders are not doing their job properly, then, well, you get what you get.

Sometimes I have experienced terrible Service. If it is from an older person who has just lost their enthusiasm for their work or is just waiting to retire, you know, someone who is just keeping the chair warm, I feel no sympathy for them at all. But when I experience young people getting it wrong, I feel so sorry for them. I feel sorry for them because they clearly do not have the leader they deserve. So often I see customers criticising these young people when it is not really their fault. If they are not being trained well, if their leader is not there with them every day, being the role model, encouraging them, you cannot blame them for not being good.

The important thing to remember also is that everyone has to have a positive attitude about what they are doing and what they want to create. If you really want to do something you can do it. You have to be positive. If you are always negative you achieve nothing. Again, leaders play a role in this, from recruitment to training to daily management.'

'But you seem to have worked most of it out for yourself.'

'Actually I have learnt many things from many people but, yes, I am lucky because Service is my nature. For me, being with guests is the easy bit. To get to that time, to the actual Service, requires a lot of work; cleaning, preparing, managing the environment; all the things the guests never see.'

These are things that he has graciously allowed me to see. I have watched those who deliver Service do everything that is required of them to make sure that The Waterside Inn is ready to receive guests, the performers dressing their own stage. Their attention to detail and sense of purpose is unfaltering. Diego checks consistently. They are always under his microscope.

In the morning staff prepare the restaurant in near silence. Cutlery and glasses are checked for cleanliness and positioned precisely. There is a sense of calm and order that is in some way reminiscent of the preparations in a holy building prior to a very different kind of Service. Here ritual combines with practicality. Everyone plays their role precisely. They go about their tasks with a practised ease that speaks of endless repetition and experience, and yet they do so in a manner that suggests the importance of a special, unique event. The room offers the promise of peace on a gentle undercurrent of controlled urgency. This is preparation before performance of the very highest order. And it is like this whether Diego is in the room watching or not.

'The location and the environment are both vital parts of Service,' Diego notes. 'To keep your environment pristine is essential and it is very, very hard work. If, for example, you go into a shop and it is tatty and dirty, then you get a bad first impression and you do not stay. The setting, the internal environment, and also the location of every business are very important. In a restaurant cleanliness and comfort are essential. However, we must also remember the purpose of a restaurant; the shape of the plates or the design of the chairs, these are not *the* most important things, but they do play their part in creating the overall experience. Not every business can be in the perfect location, but every business should remember the way location influences their guests and they should do their best to manage it well.'

I had come to appreciate whilst researching *Five Essential Ingredients for Business Success,* that location can motivate staff and further their sense of belonging, whilst also firing the imagination and expectations of guests. Diego is fully aware that his guests arrive with high expectations. He appreciates that location, perception and imagination are three of the key elements that fuse together to establish reputation. He knows how easily reputation can be lost. The Service he creates and leads is designed to surpass these expectations and fit congruently into the peaceful, riverside location.

The Waterside Inn is at the end of a road that leads only to the river Thames. There is nowhere else to go without swimming. Service begins with the greeting of Oliver, the literally long-standing doorman waiting to welcome guests, park their cars and, most importantly, begin the process of immersing them in the Waterside rather than the river.

Once inside the building two elements combine to create and reinforce this immersion. The first of these is the way and the frequency with which members of staff greet guests as they are led inwards. This is a deliberate process designed not only to provide a welcome, but more importantly to draw them into a new world –the world of The Waterside Inn – in as few paces as possible.

'When guests are with us,' Diego explains, 'we want them to be able to focus completely on their reasons for being here, whatever they may be. To do this they need to feel that they are away from their normal world; that they are in a separate and welcoming place. Creating this feeling is an important part of Service.'

I reflect for a moment on the fact that whenever I enter a business or, indeed, contact them in any way, I am entering their world. Ideally I should be able to identify their purpose, their values, the positive ways they differ from other businesses, by how they behave and by the environments they have created and operate within. And by how these make me *feel*.

I turn my thoughts back to The Waterside Inn. In the restaurant itself the patio doors that form the river-facing wall are opened whenever the weather allows, letting nature merge with the measured management of the dining experience. The front-of-house team invariably move around the room with the same apparent ease as the swans glide past outside. The birds are more likely to be noticed however.

I note,

> Location and environment influence the perceptions, expectations and feelings of guests. This is why they play such an important part in the Service experience. In fact, if they are good enough they

can even help distract guests from all the work that is going on around them. They help create the great Service illusion.

When I finish writing, I return to something Diego has just said. 'Tell me, why is engaging with guests the easy bit for you?'

'Because it is my background. I have grown up looking after people. As I say, it is my nature and when you do something that is your nature you are always relaxed. That means you can deal with anything that happens because you are in such a good state. To be honest, I can solve any problem when I am like this. Sometimes I am not even sure how it is that I know what to do; it just comes to me very quickly. So I am always comfortable in the restaurant with guests. It is my home. Obviously, without my team I am nothing. I need them. Then, when I am on the floor, I can look around and see so many different types of people and I feel good. It is never heavy on my shoulders. The day I feel that it is, is the day I stop.'

I can't help but glance at his shoulders. They look completely relaxed. An hour later when I watch him lead the pre-Service briefing his posture is different. Still relaxed, but more erect, more deliberate somehow. It is at this briefing, held before every Service begins, that Diego shares with the team the knowledge they need to have about who is eating with them, their names, where they will be sitting, their reasons for being there, and any special dietary requirements. He also reviews the team's most recent performance, providing constructive criticism and praise as required. There is no discussion. There is no debate.

'The briefing is another way I make everyone feel part of the team,' Diego says to me afterwards.

While he talks staff stand silently in a semi-circle, speaking only when asked a question. He switches languages effortlessly and swiftly as he communicates with individuals from different countries. It is not the only change in his delivery. The pace, tone, volume and energy in his voice reflect the fact that the briefing is the final part of the team's preparation. His language is precise, to the point, focused only on the upcoming Service and the standards he expects. It is the clipped language of clear direction, stripped of all non-essentials, seemingly impossible to misunderstand. It is the language that is used throughout each Service, when time for communication is minimal and yet constant information sharing is paramount. The staff make their notes. The briefing ends. It is almost time to begin. The nervous tension is palpable.

'It feels like being backstage just a few minutes before a show starts.' I admit to him.

He nods. 'Every day when I arrive here, I think to myself, Two more shows – a matinee and an evening performance.'

Diego likens himself to the conductor of a great orchestra. He directs. He orchestrates. 'During Service,' he says, 'everybody here is in tune. In an orchestra some people play violins, some play the cello, some the trombone and so on. They are like my waiters. Some serve the bread, some serve the wine, some the cheese. I don't have a stick like a maestro with an orchestra. I don't stand alone in the middle. Instead, I am floating around. I see things my staff cannot see, so I can give them direction.'

For only the second time I don't quite agree with him. I don't think that he is like the conductor of an orchestra, because an orchestra follows a score. An orchestra can rehearse precisely ahead of time. There are no surprises for the musicians when they step on to the stage at The Last Night of The Proms. Everyone knows every note they are going to play and when.

In a restaurant, and, indeed, in every other Service setting I can think of, the performance is more a form of improvisation, in which professionals seek to get in tune with their customers. For me, this makes the performance of Diego and his team all the more impressive.

I note,

He is certainly at the centre of the Service. His interactions with guests are obvious; his direction of the team far less so. He clearly uses his presence, his *character*, to keep the attention of the guests away from the work that is going on around them. He is an illusionist...Floating around...

I'm not sure when he mentions 'floating' if he is deliberately referring to his physical or mental state, or a combination of the two. Having watched him repeatedly it does seem that wherever he is and whatever he is doing physically, his mind and body are somehow in tune with everything that is going on around him. Diego would have been a great schoolteacher, not just because he likes to serve and he likes to teach, but also because he's got 20-20 vision in the back of his head!

I remember what he said about being able to solve any problem but not always being consciously aware of how he does it. My friends who are Sport Psychologists would call these *flow experiences*. Athletes would describe them as *being in the zone*. Flow experiences are the study of much academic research.[7] Essentially they are most likely to occur when a person has clear goals, feedback is immediate, challenges and skills are balanced, and their attention is fully invested. At such times the conscious sense of self disappears and with it distracting thoughts and irrelevant feelings. We are most likely to experience *flow* when doing things that we really, really enjoy.

My note reads,

Service and *flow*. If you want to serve someone brilliantly, you have to be in the zone.

In Diego's world this means giving all of your attention to someone else, to your guest. It means being so skilled that you can perform all the technical aspects of your role without conscious thought, because only then can you focus fully

---

7 If you want to know more the work of Mihaly Csikszentmihalyi is a great place to start.

on the person you are serving. I realise now that when he talks about the invisibility of great Service and the need to be able to read the minds of guests he is implying a physical and emotional state as well as a skill set. In fact, the state underpins the skill set. The state, as we now know, grows out of a genuine desire to please.

I refer back to my earlier notes when Diego said, 'Great Service is when you don't see it, but it is there. You don't have to ask for anything.' And then, a little later,

'Great Service is underpinned by the staff's ability to read people's minds, quickly and continually.'

The connection between the two is now clear. Guests shouldn't need to ask because the staff should have read their mind. I suspect that this particular piece of magic is based on the giving of skilled attention. When I ask, Diego confirms this to be the case.

'With experience you learn how to "recognise" people even before you talk to them. This is not necessarily by how they dress. Very often you can learn much from their expressions, how they look at you, how they shake your hand, the language they use. Guests always show you how they expect people to behave towards them and when around them. Some people like to ask for Service; some just like to receive it. When you understand this you can enter their world accurately.

For example, if some people drop their spectacles, they will never move to pick them up – they are used to others doing it for them. Others will automatically reach for them. There is a different way to treat each guest. We all need individual care.

Our task is to recognise this and then provide it.'

I find myself drawn by the notion that great Service is a three-step process:

1) Understand the other person and their needs fully
2) Enter their world
3) Serve.

I find myself shaking my head as I silently replay two of my more recent Service encounters. And I'm using the word *encounter* deliberately. A couple of weeks ago, on my way home from the gym, I went into a gent's outfitter to begin my search for a new suit. I was wearing jogging bottoms and a sweatshirt at the time. The fact that not one of the staff spoke to me was not the issue. Frankly, when I'm buying clothes I like to be left alone until I've either made up my mind or have a specific question to ask. No, that wasn't the problem. It was the *look* I received from the manager. It was one of those up-and-down looks accompanied by a pulling and a rising of a variety of facial muscles. The point he was making was clear. He might as well have walked up to me and demanded, 'What do you think you are doing coming into my shop dressed like that?' I felt obliged to have a cursory look around and then left. When I returned the next day dressed in a suit and tie, the same manager welcomed me warmly. He clearly didn't recognise me as the customer in the sweatshirt, and he clearly thought that I was someone more worthy of his store and his time. We chatted briefly. I bought nothing. I left feeling quietly vindicated. And subsequently told everyone I know how bad the Service is in this particular store. The 'spread' of reputation again, this time negative.

A few days later I had reason to phone a call centre. I was born in the 1950s so conversations don't start well for me if they begin with someone asking for the year of my birth. I'm trying to forget my age. I don't want reminding. Neither do I want to be reduced to a series of numbers. It gets worse still when I remember the name of the person I am talking to and they forget mine. And then they inform me that the problem we are discussing cannot be resolved because of *the system*. As if that is some other worldly, all-powerful entity. When in fact it is a process created and controlled by the humans who work in the business. Systems should serve us, not the other way round. Neither should they be an excuse for not having to develop great, or even competent Service skills.

My How-To-Deliver-Great-Service poster that I think should be on the wall of every office in every business is really taking shape in my mind. So far it reads:

Customers are people who put their trust in *you*!

To be worthy of it:

1) Understand them and their needs fully
2) Enter their world and prove that you have a desire to please
3) Serve with a genuine smile on your face.

I would quite like to have included *Learn to become invisible and to read minds*, but I think that would be too much too soon. On the other hand, maybe that is the way to promote a change in attitudes towards Service? Maybe I should be suggesting that the power that comes from great Service – and there is an undeniable power – is something akin to the power of the Jedi? Perhaps my Let's Get Better at Service campaign should be fronted by Yoda saying, 'Service a great power it has. May the Service be with you.' You understand why I don't work in advertising.

Service has a power because it affects people. It influences how they feel and how they behave. At its best it remains a positive talking point and memory long after it happens. The very best Service is unique in that its power does come from a form of invisibility, skills and processes that go unnoticed by the guests and yet play a pivotal role in creating a great experience.

Service has power because it affects us *emotionally*. Brilliant Service makes us feel that we matter, that we are understood, and that the people we are engaging with actually *care* about us. It creates a positive connection. Brilliant Service can actually make us feel brilliant! It makes us want to reward it. Brilliant Service influences brilliantly because it brings to bear the powers of likeness, reciprocity, commitment and consistency and, because it is so rare, scarcity.

I write,

Service is far more than just selling, even though it is integral to it. Service actually has a purpose of its own, which is to make you feel great; to make you feel understood and valued. We might get an emotional thrill when buying certain products, but when Service is good we *always* feel wonderful.

This only happens when the professionals can recognise their guests starting point, their current reality, and meet them there. It only happens when the Service professionals are willing to make that journey with a genuine smile on their face. And this act of meeting guests in their world doesn't just happen at the start of Service. It occurs throughout.

A step in the right direction and an atmosphere that reveals all

From Diego's perspective every table in the restaurant is an individual world. The guests at each table are there for their own reasons and have their own expectations of what constitutes great Service. On top of this, their mood might also change as the hours pass. This means that the front-of-house staff have only a few paces – the space between tables – to shift their focus fully from one world to the next, to assess whether or not it is appropriate to speak whilst serving, to remember what they last talked about, to remind themselves of anything Diego might have said at the pre-briefing about the guests they are approaching. After each interaction they also have to decide if there is information that needs to be shared immediately and, if so, with whom.

Information sharing is essential to the provision of great Service.[8] At The Waterside Inn this starts with the pre-Service briefing and continues throughout and beyond each Service. Diego always provides feedback about the team and individual performances and also shares lessons learnt about and from the guests.

'Communication is like Service itself,' he says. 'Too much is as bad as not enough. As you know, the briefings I hold are short and straight to the point. When I brief the staff before each Service I never repeat myself.

Now, feedback from the guests is also very important. Often guests will write or email to say what a wonderful time they have had. Once in a while they will make a complaint. I do reply personally to all forms of feedback.'

I decide that my next question should be both simple and stark. 'How do you manage mistakes?'

He accepts it with the same grace that he does a compliment. The only difference being that if I had just offered a compliment he would have made an immediate reference to the quality of his team. With this, though, he makes it personal. Even here, even now, he is protecting his staff from any sense of external criticism.

'I always takes responsibility and blame myself for every

---

8 During my recent call centre encounter I had to repeat the entire story about the problem I was experiencing, even though I had done so in two previous communications.

The Diego Masciaga Way

error,' he says. 'Of course, we all wish that we did not make mistakes. That is what we are striving to achieve every Service. However, we are human beings at the end of the day. We are not perfect.'

He makes the point softly, delicately.

We are human beings at the end of the day...

It is a phrase he has used so many times, always to make the same point, always to explain why perfection cannot be reached. Some people, I fear, would use it as an excuse for mediocrity. Diego uses it to emphasise the challenge in seeking perpetual excellence, the courage that is needed to pursue an ideal.

'The biggest mistake,' he continues, 'is not following up and doing something great to compensate for the original error. You see, the best opportunity for creating a great friend of your business is when someone complains. We have very few complaints, but when we do 99 per cent go on to become our friends. Businesses should avoid thinking that they have given a gift by saying 'Sorry'. Instead they should keep their eyes on the guests until they leave and make it great throughout. It isn't just what you say and do in these situations that matters, you also have to get the timing right. Timing is as important when talking to guests as it is when talking to staff. If I see that a guest is unhappy I will assess what is happening and decide whether or not it is best to wait a while before speaking to them.

In the same way, if I decide that I have to tell off a member of the team I will wait for the right time. It is no good telling someone off during Service because they are already working too hard to be able to accept it and learn from it in that moment. It is better to wait for a day or two until they are calm. Then it is necessary to pick the right place. Sometimes, for example, I will talk to them when they are on their own doing a task in the garden. It should always be private.'

'Following on from that, Diego, I think one of the most frequently debated questions regarding Service is this one: is the guest always right?'

'This is a very big question. For me, the guest is always right up to a point. If they start to become rude they are not a guest anymore, they're just being a horrible human being, so even if they are paying they are not then our guest. You see, selfish people will take advantage of staff. They will try to make the staff feel like a doormat. If you go into any business and look only for the bad you will always find it. Everywhere! Even in the best places you can always find the negative if you really look for it. By doing that you make the staff really stressed. If a client is rude to me I will never be rude back. You still have to treat people respectfully. But I will not accept anyone being rude to my staff. Never! You see, in the end, if the customer is always right and can behave however they choose you can no longer call what you do a profession. And what we do is a very serious profession.'

I write,

Diego and his team demonstrate their understanding of individual guests by what they say, or don't say, to them. Listening is vital, but so is looking and interpreting. Managing communication is an essential part of Service. This is especially true in the aftermath of a mistake.

Overall, the moral seems to be: the more you know about someone the easier mind reading becomes; the more capable you are of meeting your guests' Service needs; the more likely you are to turn them into friends of your business.

Diego accepts this as a statement of the obvious. 'Yes. The more we understand our guests the better we can serve them. Sometimes that means realising that certain guests hardly ever want to speak to us. Sometimes it means knowing that they like to have conversations with different staff. Understanding your guests is far more than just knowing what food they like, or what they might be allergic to. That is basic. Understanding your guests means understanding what pleases them. Some guests, for example, have been coming here for many years and have never looked at a menu! They like it if I choose for them. I ask them how they are feeling, what they are in the mood to eat, and then they trust me to choose the dishes. Obviously, many other people want to make their own decisions.

The second part in understanding our guests is remembering what we have learnt. Many of our guests return to us. Some visit on a regular basis, others only for very special occasions. No matter, we have to remember who they are and what they like. Most importantly, every time they return we have to understand how they are feeling *today*. We must never think that we know them so well we no longer need to give them our attention. In the kitchen the chefs give the food their absolute attention. In the restaurant we do the same with our guests.'

Diego stops. His smile returns. He has been talking quickly, with urgency. It isn't just because this topic is important to him. Everything we have talked about is important to him. It seems rather that we are now at the very heart of the matter. Everything else, the recruitment, the training, his leadership, they are all designed to increase the chances of Service being brilliant. In essence, it all seems to boil down to one simple question:

How good are we making our guests feel today?

This apparently simple question is crammed with complexity. To repeatedly make your guests feel great, whilst maintaining a very profitable business, requires skills of the highest level. These include knowing when to talk to guests and what to talk about.

'Diego, when you are talking to guests how do you know what to talk about?'

'Aah, this is interesting because it isn't just knowing what to talk about, but also just as importantly knowing *how* to talk about it. Like everything else we do, this needs preparation.

You see, as you know some guests like to talk and there's only so much you can say about the food, the weather and the swans. So you let the guests choose. With a particular guest I can only talk about certain topics, with another guest a different topic. If they want to talk about politics, about geography, about the economic state of the world or about sport, you simply follow their lead. This means that you need to have knowledge and I drill into my staff how important it is to read. You cannot buy knowledge; you have to work at it.'

By around 11am most mornings Diego is ready to have his own early lunch. Whilst he eats he reads a newspaper, updating himself on any topic that guests are likely to raise when talking to him. At night, when he arrives home, he will also check the latest news before going to bed.

I add to my previous note,

> Remembering is as important as listening and looking when it comes to managing conversations with guests. Service staff need more than just their own technical expertise; they also need up-to-date general knowledge to be able to converse about any topic.

'Diego, you said that knowing *how* to talk to guests is as important as knowing what to talk about it. What do you mean by that?'

'You always have to be on the step below your guest,' he says. 'By this I mean that you should never say or do anything that makes your guest feel foolish or makes them think that they do not know much. This is true even when talking about food or wine. Some guests ask questions and want to learn. Some want to share with you what they know. It is our job to accommodate both. After all, how can you please your guests, make them feel very good, if you behave as if you are obviously superior to them? Guests will not feel comfortable and relaxed if staff communicate to them like that. It is obvious. So, when I talk to a guest about what they want to talk about I am able to do two things. One, I can meet them on their terms. Two, I am not going to know as much as they do. I have probably read something about it or seen it on the news, but now we are talking about a subject they understand very well so I am, once again, a step below the guest.'

I note,

He operates one step ahead of his team and one step below his guests; both determined by the position from which he can best serve.

I am drawn back to the memory of the young female sales assistant who objected to me thanking her for her Service. I don't know the precise words Diego is going to use to answer my next question, but I am pretty sure of the direction he will take.

'Does being a step below mean that guests are somehow superior to you; that those who provide Service are lower down a social scale than the people they serve?'

'No! Let me say this very clearly. Clearing a plate, for example, is not demeaning even for me and I am the boss. Actually I am proud to do something like that because it gives me an opportunity to have contact with the guest and they often tell me how much they appreciate that. Staff need to be taught that when you are talking to a guest how you stand is important. If you stand with dignity and personality, if you are clean and well dressed, the guest will see you as a professional. This is how it should be.'

I tell him of my experience with the young sales assistant. I ask him what advice he would give to her.

'She might think that she is good at sales without ever realising that she is actually providing the Service of selling.' His face hardens as he speaks. It quickly becomes obvious that it is the topic not the behaviour of the young woman that is making him so serious. 'You see, too often in this country Service becomes mistaken for servant. This is very wrong. People who provide Service are not servants. To me, a person who behaves like a servant is like a doormat. They are willing to be treated in any way. My staff are not, and never will be, servants. And I will not allow anyone to treat them as if they are. They are dignified, skilled people with good general knowledge and a pride in what they do. They are passionate and committed professionals.'

It is true. I have spent many hours watching the team at work, before and during Service. Like all elite teams they know how preparation influences performance. They prepare thoroughly. They attend rigorously to the tiniest details. No matter what they are doing their individual personalities always shine through. And whenever they see a guest they smile.

Frédéric Poulette told me, 'The most important thing I have learnt from Mr Diego is to smile, to be happy. You have to be happy with what you are doing. If you want to achieve something and you are not happy you won't reach it, you will not be willing to give 100 per cent.'

It isn't just shared behaviours that join the staff together. Diego insists on the wearing of a team uniform.

'I like my team to be dressed the same,' he tells me. 'A uniform makes everyone equal. Without it, some people might come to work wearing more expensive clothes than someone else in the team. I don't want this. Secondly, it is important for the guests to see all staff looking the same, it gives the restaurant identity. The uniform is very casual in the morning because we do our own cleaning here, so everyone is involved in that. Before Service starts the staff put on their more formal uniform. For me, it is very important that this uniform is not too over-the-top. I have been to some restaurants and some shops too, where staff wear very expensive uniforms, suits by top designers for example. I think this is a mistake. Not every guest in these restaurants and shops will be able to afford such clothes. So when they see that the staff are better dressed than they are, they might feel put down because of it. This means the staff that are there to serve are now one step above the guest instead of one step below. Some of my staff own expensive jewellery and watches. I

The Diego Masciaga Way

always ask them not to wear these during Service for this reason.

Different members of the team wear different uniforms. This helps the guests to recognise what their role is and who has the most responsibility. Although, of course, beyond their uniform the staff in charge should demonstrate this through how they behave. Again, uniforms and cleanliness reflect dignity. We are not an army, but we must be presentable and organised in front of our guests. This is true at all times and not just in the restaurant.'

The way he says that prompts the following question, 'Diego, what *is* a restaurant?'

He doesn't smile at me, but he does look as if he has to stop himself. 'A restaurant,' he says, 'is a place in which guests can become lost in each other and their reasons for being there. To make this happen you must allow the guests to relax and feel comfortable. If you think about it, the first part of the word *restaurant* is *rest*. So a restaurant must have an environment in which guests can rest and feel good. Then staff can meet their needs in the ways that each guest most appreciates.'

Whilst Diego leaves me briefly to take an unexpected phone call, I look up the meaning of the word *restaurant* in a dictionary. I read *'a place where meals are prepared and served to customers'*. I so much more prefer Diego's definition! I would much sooner be *lost* in my reasons for sharing time with someone else than be simply sat in a meal production outlet.

Ruth Reichl, the American food writer, wrote, 'Pull up a chair. Take a taste. Come join us. Life is endlessly delicious.' In the world according to Diego, Service helps makes it so. The restaurant is the place where guests can be immersed in their own life. It is the place where more than the food can be delicious.

As I consider this I realise my next question. When Diego returns I ask,

'Tell me, why do you always refer to them as guests rather than customers?'

This time he lets his smile show. 'A customer is someone who comes out to eat, drink, pay and go. That's it. A guest does the same but you welcome them as if you are welcoming them into your home. You open your door to your guest as if you are at home. The Waterside Inn is my (working) home. This is how I feel when I am here. If you come to my family home, I want to please you and I will get pleasure out of it. When you visit us here it is the same.'

On reflection, we have gone right back to the very beginning. It is the attitude of the staff, their understanding of Service and their desire to please that creates a guest; that differentiates them from a customer in the professional's mind. I'm beginning to think that I should change my Service poster, that I should use the word 'guest' instead of 'customer'. After all, you can argue that even in the virtual world of the Internet, people who visit a website can be thought of as guests. There is an obvious challenge here, though. I don't think it would lay in making more businesses use the word 'guest'. I think it would be in making their staff *feel* just what the word means and using that feeling to guide all their behaviours.

Talking of behaviours, I have another question. 'Diego, what are the processes of Service here? Who does what?'

'The restaurant is divided into two sections,' he explains, marking out space in the air with either hand. 'In each section there is a maître d'hôtel in charge. Each has a no.2, called a chef de rang. They make sure that the right cutlery is placed on the table, the food is ordered at the pass, and so on. They are supported by a commis who clears the plates, a runner who brings the dishes in from the kitchen, a member of staff who serves the water and a Sommelier in charge of the wine. There is always a senior member of staff at the front door, welcoming guests. This is a priority. This has to be someone who knows our guests and understands them. Often I do this. It lets me see why guests are here today and how they are feeling when they arrive. If the person at the front door gets this wrong, everything can go – how would you call it? – Pear-shaped.

In my role I have to keep my personality, too. I have to keep my head on my shoulders. I always have to be calm and controlled. If the leader ever becomes emotional during Service then it will damage performance. As we have already discussed the leader can influence their team very easily. Under pressure, the leader must always set the example.'

I pursue his regimented approach for just a moment

longer. 'Apart from you everyone has clearly defined duties that they don't go beyond?

'Everyone has their role, their place. This is necessary to ensure a coordinated Service. Everyone also has to know how to act, look, move and talk. They have to know how to do this well even if they are not quite feeling like it. During Service we are all performing together, but during that time the staff are not allowed to chat with each other. They are not there to socialise. They must always show that they are enjoying what they are doing, even if they are not busy at that moment. Most importantly, I want my staff to think further than their feet. They have to go the extra mile whilst staying within their agreed boundaries. Sometimes during Service I keep in the background, giving the team freedom to show what they can do. Then I go into the restaurant later to check.'

I note,

> Think further than your feet. What a wonderful way to describe going the extra mile!

I think back to the conversation we had so long ago now about the different ways that staff are rewarded for their commitment and effort. One reward they are not guaranteed is Service charge. Diego does not demand a compulsory payment from guests. They reward Service only if they choose to. I ask him why he is against the addition of a Service charge.

'Because once staff know they will make 10 per cent or

more extra before they even begin to talk to their guest it is easier for them not to care, to think only of their financial reward. That threatens the very nature of Service, of being motivated by a desire to please. Secondly, if you get an unexpected tip for doing something that gives you great pleasure it is worth more than a compulsory Service charge – you get personal pleasure and you get a reward from the guest! The guests must always feel, they must always know, that we are not here just to take their money. We want firstly to make guests feel great, remembering too that the bottom line is that we are a business.'

I plan to come back to the very significant issue of Service and business success another time. Right now I am wondering how great Service manifests itself. If it is based on invisibility and never having to ask how do you recognise it? My mind trips back briefly to the two inter-related questions I asked myself early on in my study.[9] Then I return to the question at hand.

'You say that Service is about pleasing guests, making them feel great. How do you know when you have achieved this?'

'The atmosphere in the restaurant is the immediate source of feedback,' he says. His left hand straightens his tie. He falls silent briefly. He looks as he often does before he speaks as if he is reliving scenes from the restaurant in his

9 They were: Does everything have a shape? If so, what shape does brilliant Service have?

mind's eye. When he has seen enough he goes on, 'the perfect atmosphere is when you hear guests laughing and talking, you see them smiling and having an enjoyable time. There should be a feeling of warmth. A restaurant is not a church or a temple. You don't go to a restaurant to contemplate the food. You go there to share with people.

As professionals we have to put our soul into Service to create the atmosphere. If Service is sterile, guests will never come back. If the restaurant is too quiet, for example, it is my job to raise the atmosphere. I am not saying that it should be too loud either. Again, it is about getting the balance right. If it is too quiet guests become afraid to talk; they whisper to each other. They can become tense. This is the opposite of what we want our guests to experience. After all, when we were born we were natural and relaxed, not stiff and tense. So we should be natural and relaxed in a restaurant. Also remember what I said about the importance of a senior member of the team greeting guests at the front door. When people arrive you can see or feel their mood. Sometimes they are not in a good mood. If you have a very good atmosphere in the restaurant, even guests who are not in a good mood will change; the atmosphere will influence them. They are human beings so they cannot resist it. My advice to all people who provide Service to others is create the right atmosphere. This is vital. If you cannot do this, you cannot win.'

My note reads,

You have to know what atmosphere you want to create. You have to know how to manage it. Atmosphere is a powerful source of influence.

I think my How-To-Deliver-Great-Service poster should include an instruction about ensuring the right atmosphere.

To ask a professional, 'What kind of atmosphere do you want to create for your guests?' is to ask one of those questions that is loaded to bursting point, because they have to know not only *why* that is the best atmosphere for their guests, but also *how* to create it and control it.

Having said that, it does seem to me that whenever you get a group of people together atmosphere is inevitable. It seems equally obvious that atmosphere influences emotion and behaviour. Someone, therefore, has to lead and manage the atmosphere that is created whenever Service professionals and guests interact. I will suggest, as a final obvious piece on this topic, that someone needs to be a Service professional.

I realise that I have observed Diego at work in this regard. As I review my time in the restaurant I recall having seen him change the pitch, tone and volume of his conversation with guests to either match or lead the atmosphere in the room. I have seen him put guests new to The Waterside Inn at their ease in a matter of minutes.

As I look back through the notes I have made I find that I have commented on the fact that there always seems to be a happy atmosphere in the restaurant; a level of noise that suggests that everyone is fully engaged in their own conversations and that gives you permission to do the same. With my final comment and question for the day we both acknowledge that I am asking for clarification and not seeking revelation.

'Diego, I have seen guests pay their bill and then sit in the restaurant or outside by the river for an hour or more.'

'Yes?'

'When do they stop being your guest?'

'When they leave. The guest is our guest until they leave not until they pay. If a guest pays the bill at 2pm and then sits there until 4pm the last 2 hours have to be as good as everything before they paid. The ending of the service is very, very important.'

Indeed. It is all too easy for me to think of establishments in which the staff lost interest in me once they had my money. I have even walked out of some restaurants having paid the bill without anyone speaking to me, in marked contrast to their apparent enthusiasm when I walked in. It is just another one of those indicators that marks the difference between a guest and a customer. After all, you would never allow a guest to leave your home ignored and in silence. Would you?

I begin writing my summary notes alone in the summerhouse. I am not in a rush to leave. And no one is in a rush to make me. I settle in and let my mind wander over everything Diego has said and all that I have experienced here. I have barely written a hundred words when a smiling young man appears with a fresh pot of Earl Grey tea.

I hadn't asked for it.

The Diego Masciaga Way

Summary

Service has a power because it affects people emotionally. It influences how they feel and how they behave. At its best it remains a positive talking point and a memory long after it happens. Outstanding Service is unique in that the skills and processes of the professionals involved tend to go unnoticed by the guest.

The lessons are:

Lesson no. 1

Thorough preparation and planning precede the delivery of outstanding Service. Everyone involved in the delivery of Service needs to be highly skilled at their role; they need to understand that they are always at work, always *performing*, when guests are present. The aim of such preparation and planning is to deliver Service that is simply excellent.

Lesson no. 2

The environment plays an important part in determining the quality of Service and in creating a first impression. The environment is more than just internal decoration. It is also how well the business fits into its location. In a restaurant cleanliness and comfort are essential. Environments need to be rigorously managed and maintained on a daily basis.

Lesson no. 3

To provide outstanding bespoke Service, professionals have to understand their guests' current reality. This includes their needs, their mood and their expectations. These can all change during the interaction. Service professionals, therefore, need to think further than their feet; they need to be giving skilled attention to their guests at all times.

Lesson no. 4

Mistakes happen. A mistake is a great opportunity to create a new life-long friend for your business. The biggest mistake lies in not doing something great to compensate for the original error. An apology is not a gift. It is a starting point. Timing is as important in managing mistakes as it is in every other aspect of Service; staff have to know not only what to say and do to provide compensation but *when* to say and do it.

Lesson no. 5

Welcome guests not customers. Welcome them as if you are welcoming them into your home. The difference between a guest and a customer lies in the attitude of staff, in their understanding of Service and their desire to please. Ensure that people are treated as guests for as long as they are with you – not just until they pay. Say farewell to your guests as enthusiastically as you greet them.

Lesson no. 6

Feedback is vital. Atmosphere is the most immediate and important form of feedback. Atmosphere influences emotions and behaviours. It is important, therefore, to know precisely what kind of atmosphere you need to create and how to do so. Professionals take the lead in creating and maintaining the desired atmosphere.

∾

5

LONGEVITY, CONSISTENCY AND IMPROVEMENT

The habit of excellence

࿔

'We are what we repeatedly do.
Excellence, then, is not an act, but a habit.'
Aristotle

Variety, sparkle and the size of the red carpet

Every morning Diego Masciaga arrives at work at around 9.30am. He likes to vary his entrance.

'Sometimes,' he says, 'I come in through the front door. Sometimes I come in from the back. My staff know this is not to catch them out; rather it helps me to keep a fresh perspective, to see if things are out of place. If you enter a building through the same door every day you become used to seeing things in a certain way, you can become lazy. I cannot afford that.'

It is spring 2014. This is our second meeting of the year. We are coming towards the end of our time together. Just a few more interviews in the summerhouse. Just a few more hours of observation. Then, for me, the time to write it all up. For Diego, business as normal.

Although as has been established, that doesn't mean the endless repetition of the same routines. Diego is a man who likes coming at things from different angles; who values variety and understands the need for constant improvement.

'If I did the same routine every day I would get bored,' he says without any prompting from me. 'This place still gives me a lot of excitement. I think I still have a lot to do here. The day that you say you can't improve any more is the day you should just stay at home and fall asleep. So, for me, there must be improvement every day, even just improvements in small details. You cannot let things fall down. If they fall down it is difficult to get them back up again.'

Whether he knows it or not, in his first two comments Diego has graciously opened the door to my final topic for discussion,

Just how have you managed to stay at the top for so long?

At the time of writing The Waterside Inn has held the most prestigious culinary awards for nearly three decades. Diego has been providing world class Service for as long. Becoming a world leader is a rare achievement. Maintaining that status for any length of time is even more impressive. Turning it into an accepted part of who you are is something altogether different. Something even more special. I want to know what the rest of us can learn about how to create longevity, consistency and continual improvement.

Diego hasn't even sipped at his espresso yet and he has already touched on:

- Routine versus variety
- The importance of excitement
- The need for gradual, continual improvements
- The need to avoid even the slightest lowering of standards

I decide to address them in that order. 'Diego, why are variety and spontaneity so important in maintaining your success?'

'To be honest with you, I value the power of spontaneity!' Diego straightens abruptly, his mood changing in an instant. Suddenly he is energised. His eyes are twinkling. He slaps his right palm against his thigh. 'Often I change routines here for the staff without warning. Some elements, of course, you need to plan ahead. Some things you don't. Actually, some things you shouldn't! It makes things really come alive for both me and my staff! If you change on the spot it takes far more energy and effort to get it right and it is a tiring thing to do. The benefit though is that it guarantees that we are all very alert. You see, when you get used to a routine, you miss many things. This is because routines dull the mind and you need to stimulate your mind every day when you arrive at work. Sometimes rules are there to be broken if you want to achieve and maintain the highest levels.'

Now he reaches for his coffee. He doesn't look as if he needs it though. For my part my mind is racing, keeping up with his sudden burst of enthusiasm. The way he clearly differentiates between routine and habit is fascinating and instructive. Whilst there are many established processes here, the only real habit that Diego and his team are committed to is the creation of process and outcome excellence.

He is fully aware of the dangers fuelled by the rigid adherence to habits created by set routines. He knows that you cannot provide Service excellence if your mind is dull. He uses spontaneity to help teach his staff how to think creatively, to adapt to the unexpected, and to think further than their feet. They can trust him not only to develop, support, critique and guide them, but also to introduce changes, challenges and problems for them to address. On the one hand, everything here is done by the book. On the other hand, the book has innumerable blank pages upon which Diego can write whatever he chooses. It is another insight into this culture of excellence.

I wonder if it is also one of the ways he seeks to ensure excitement amongst his team.

'Yes, it is. Let me say again, routines destroy sparkle. Staff should always have a sparkle of excitement when they work. Businesses cannot survive and grow without happy staff who are excited by what they do. Every day I will talk to the people in my team individually to help create this. Then the very act of providing Service should be exciting. Every Service is unique. Therefore there can be no routine way of providing it. It is new every time. It is easy to be excited when you are doing something new, isn't it? Particularly when it is something that you have chosen to do because you think it is important.

The final thing is that as soon as I feel that a member of the team is ready to move on, I help them to leave. This is good for them because it helps them to progress their career and it is good for me because it means they leave before their excitement at being here disappears.'

My note reads,

The sparkle and excitement of Service! What a wonderful way to describe both how the interaction should be and the attitude Diego expects from his team.

It is interesting to note that Diego recognises the importance of helping staff to move on at the right time, and the right time is *before* they demonstrate a loss of enthusiasm for their current job. It is clear that no one in his team is allowed to stagnate, to perform without passion. His view is simply that their guests deserve better than that, and that by serving the guests well he and the team serve the business well. We have gone full circle, back to the relationship between pleasing and profit. It is time now, though, to be more explicit about it.

'Diego, Can you please guests and still make a good profit?'

He takes a moment before replying. I get the sense that he is once again deciding how best to sequence his answer. When he starts, he speaks without hesitation.

'In my profession, like others, I am required to sell. I sell food and wine and accommodation, but the material things alone are not enough. I also have to sell pleasure. I have to sell a great experience. If you try to take advantage of guests and over-push what you are selling, they will realise what you are doing and walk away. So you have to be honest with your guests when you sell to them. And – and this is very important – you have to make them feel comfortable in the environment and with you personally. Guests need to feel comfortable in order to have a great time and to feel confident in spending their money.

Also, it is necessary for staff to feel comfortable too. So when a company is healthy, it is essential that all staff know this. When they feel comfortable and safe it is easier for them to focus on serving their guests, because they are not secretly worrying about their own futures.

Remember that quality and money hate each other. I have to buy the best quality at the best price. However you can get the balance right. If the guest knows that they are getting value for money they will be satisfied. Sometimes you have to give a little bit, too. If you only take, take, take you are not providing great Service and you are not thinking in the long-term. When you offer something free to please a guest,

The Diego Masciaga Way

champagne for example or even something more like a trip on our boat, that can bring a guest back five times.'

He pauses momentarily. I watch him prepare the second part of his answer.

'Turnover is not as important as profit,' he says. 'It is essential to manage staff costs in order to create profit. Whenever I increase a member of the team's salary I also move them onto a different section. In that way they gain experience and skill and they are also able to multi-task. Training staff well and, in our case, teaching them to multi-task, develops them as professionals, increases their career prospects, and at the same time enables me to keep our staff costs at an appropriate level. Because only a profitable business can have a long life, I am always looking for ways to save costs whilst maintaining or raising standards.'

Diego's commitment to developing his team is, ultimately, a reflection of his commitment to the business. The man whose nature is to serve others never forgets the need to make the required profit.

'Everybody says to me that I have two personalities. Maybe it is because I am a Gemini.' He says this with the same smile that he shares with the guests. 'Everyone in the team knows that I am on their side, but also that I have to think always like a director of the company. I have to run the place as a business.'

I ask, 'How else do you manage costs?'

'By simple energy saving. The important thing here is that you can't just tell staff to switch off a light bulb, for example.

You have to make them understand why it is important and to think and feel of the place as their home – or their own business. Then they will save energy. It is also true to say that I hate waste. This is a useful trait when thinking of making a profit.' He smiles dryly this time. 'I think I need to be clear about what I mean by waste. You see, giving a guest a free drink is not waste; that is a gift that is usually rewarded. No, what I mean by waste is not managing staff properly or not managing costs properly. I do spend a lot of my time managing costs.'

I am aware that often at the end of a very long day, when the evening Service is finished, Diego retires alone to his office to balance the books. In my book, I write,

The Waterside Inn has grown during the recession and it isn't because the majority of the guests are wealthy. It is because he never stops combining brilliant Service with brilliant business.

I want to explore the role of Service in creating profitability and business longevity just a little more. 'Tell me Diego, how important is Service in creating repeat business, in ensuring survival and growth?'

'Service at the end of the day is often the key to success. Production is extremely important of course, but nowadays more and more people recognise that Service is the key. I believe that great Service is the way you create repeat business.

To be successful over a long period of time businesses

need not only to sell, but also to have clients who visit repeatedly. If you want to last you have to have regular guests coming back time after time. It is true that you have to get your guests through your front door in the first place, but then you have to look after them so well that they want to come back. It is the quality of the Service that achieves this. This can be in a shop, or selling a car, or selling insurance. It is true no matter what the business sells. The best PR or advertising comes from your guests and what they say about you. This, for me, is genuine advertising.'

It is a form of genuine advertising that certainly works for The Waterside Inn. I know of very few successful businesses that do so little marketing and advertising and yet have such an expansive and loyal customer base.

'What keeps us full all year long,' Diego continues, 'is not simply the millionaire or the billionaire. It's the people who save to come here. If a guest chooses a bottle of wine for £50 and another chooses a bottle for £10,000 you must treat both equally well. Remember that the person who paid £50 might well have saved for it. The guest who paid £10,000 may well be able to afford to buy another easily.

I train all of my team to understand and act upon the fact that here the red carpet is the same size for everyone. By this I mean we treat everyone equally well. Think of a couple, we can call them Mr. and Mrs. Brown, who can only afford to visit us once every few years for a special occasion. They cannot afford to spend as much as some of our other guests but their visit is still very special to them. That means it must be very special to us! The truth is we have an obligation to make sure they have a wonderful time. They have saved up deliberately to come here. They trust us with their money and their celebration. We have to be grateful for their trust and know how to make sure they have a great experience. The quality of Service can never be determined by how much someone might spend.'

His reference to a sense of *obligation* really catches my attention. Especially as it grows out of his sense of truth rather than a responsibility placed on him by another. In Diego's world-view the truth is that we are all obliged to serve. For him, it's not a question of should we serve, but rather where and how we do it.

John D. Rockefeller, the American business magnate and philanthropist, wrote, 'Every right implies a responsibility; every opportunity, an obligation, every possession, a duty.' Diego certainly looks for opportunities to serve. His life story has been shaped by his search for those opportunities. From a business perspective perhaps his greatest ability is the way he brings together his need to serve with his other great obligation, which is to maintain the success of the business.

Passion, positivity and timeless values

Watching Diego at work one sees two great forces, the idealism of Service and the financial realities of business, fused together in what, on the surface at least, appear to be a most harmonious marriage. I wonder if that is how it feels to him.

'Diego, how do you personally balance your beliefs about the nature and purpose of Service, and your natural desire to serve, with the realities of being successful in business? Don't you find that idealism and realism clash with each other?'

'If they did we would not have been so successful for so long,' he says with all the calm assurance of a man who knows he has the evidence to prove his point. 'If you provide great Service and surround this with good business practices, sooner or later you will become successful. You must want to provide Service because you believe in it and because you want to make people feel wonderful, not just because it makes good business sense.'

My note reads,

> Build your business around your passion. Whatever *your* passion
> is, you need to ensure you have around you people who are
> passionate about serving.

'Beyond that,' I ask, 'to what extent do you spend time planning and thinking ahead?'

His reply is immediate. 'I am always thinking and planning eight months to one year ahead. By October I get an accurate feeling for what business will be like for the next year. How do I do this? By speaking to the guests. I get insights into business and attitudes, any fears people might have about the economy and so on. I am not an economist, but at the same time I cannot sit back, especially when we as a business are doing well. If you think that life is all roses you stop preparing for problems that might happen in the future. So I am always thinking, planning, looking many months ahead.'

His lack of hesitation accurately reflects his well-honed approach for strategic thinking and planning. He finds Service a natural and obvious opportunity for strategic exploration. He manages his communication with his guests so well that he not only enhances the quality of their experience, he also gains strategic insights.

'I have to keep repeating these two things,' he continues. 'The first is that at the end of the day the business has to be profitable. The second is that money and quality don't always like each other. But if you keep your standards really high whilst controlling your outgoings, money will come eventually. It might not come quickly, but it will come. Again, you have to understand why the guest is with you. For example, if it is a working business lunch, the guests often won't spend too much. Another time, though, for the same guests money might be no object. I have to recognise that and make the most of it.'

This is more than mere opportunism. I am really beginning to see now how his philosophy that Service is pleasing opens the door for the expression of his personal values and the achieving of corporate goals.

I write,

'Service is pleasing' is at once an ethical and a pragmatic frame. It gives him permission to be welcoming, generous and caring and, at the same time, to maximise profits when the time is right. Whenever he sees that it will please a guest to spend more money, Diego has an obligation to help them. That follows on naturally: how can you be committed to Service and not be obliging? If that means helping a guest to spend significant amounts of money, then so be it.

It also means making Mr. and Mrs. Brown feel wonderful too.

Service – at the heart of a values-based business.

When I finish writing I decide to ask him just how he manages to maintain standards. He has already talked about the challenge of delivering ten performances every week, and of the hard work that goes ahead of each performance. 'On a practical level Diego, how do you maintain the same high level of quality every day?'

'The answer is very easy to say and very difficult to achieve.' He sits back before he continues. He looks as if he is opening his chest, making it easier to breathe. 'Success,' he says, 'is achieved by managing details. In every business there are always so many details. So you always have to identify these details, sometimes very little things, the things that others might miss, and improve these. You might have all the big elements of your business in place, but if some of the details are wrong, or are not as good as they could be, they will always create a negative effect. We have to remember, too that there are always ways we can improve if we look closely enough. This is the first thing.

Next the leader has to make sure that everyone in the team has the energy to perform well. I talked to you before about the importance of rest. If I see someone who is a bit run-down I talk to them. I want to understand how they are feeling and why, because you cannot maintain standards if people are too tired. If it is necessary I might give them 2 or 3 days off on full pay to recharge their batteries. But I never say it's because I can see that they are tiring. Time off from work needs to be treated as precious time. It took me maybe 10 years to learn this. If you cannot rest fully during the week, you have to rest well and fully on your days off. We are not machines; we cannot perform well if we are too tired.'

Although in my experience it is highly unusual for a business leader to send a member of staff on paid leave because they are showing signs of fatigue, it doesn't seem unusual to hear Diego say that he does. It is just another example of how he successfully combines his instinct to please and care for others (including his staff), with an absolute focus on the maintenance of excellence.

Perhaps he really does have two faces? One that looks to please people and one that looks to please the bottom line. Or perhaps they are just two expressions of the same face?

Either way, his talk about the importance of rest incorporates two very powerful messages to his staff. When he says, '...you have to rest well and fully on your days off...' he is reminding everyone that *you are going to work really hard together when you are here!* His other observation that, '...we cannot perform well if we are too tired...' sends the message, *I expect your best when you are here!*

That is what he gets. For all the reasons that he has shared with me, his staff rise to meet his expectations and the many challenges he sets. They are all fully invested in the belief that anyone can be great for a few days and that what marks them apart is their consistency over so many years. Success, though, brings with it its own risks. When I ask how he manages success, he shakes his head and glances from side to side. *He's a Gemini,* I remind myself just a split-second before he starts talking.

'Success is not easy,' he says, 'because it means you cannot afford to relax. Ever. The more successful you are the more people watch you and talk about you. The better you get the more people will notice and comment on the things you get wrong. This is a part of human nature. So you always have to be at your best. Also you always need to remember that you can disappear very quickly. I know that some people are scared of success just as some people are scared of failure. I have no fear. I have my own beliefs and personality, so I am not scared by the success we achieve. We do not do what we do here out of fear, but because we believe it is the right thing to do.'

'How do you deal with the fact that you are in a profession that is so open to public criticism and commentary?

'Sometimes it is not easy. I cope with it because I am very

positive. I always work in a positive and simple way. I am just me and this is what I do. My priority is The Waterside Inn, representing it well and making sure that the business grows. For me, The Waterside Inn comes first and myself afterwards. I hate it when I see people who are employed trying to eat in the boss's chair. By which I mean, trying to make themselves more important than the business.'

No matter how much he has his own clear views about what Service is and how it should be provided, no matter how much he is recognized as a global authority in his own right, Diego never forgets that he is an employee. He serves his boss from the same one-step-below that he serves his guests. I take us back to his previous comment about businesses disappearing. 'What makes that happen, Diego?'

'Businesses stop learning. They stop listening. They lose the excitement and enthusiasm that helped them to succeed in the first place. I have been through recessions and booms. I have seen many things change. I know that businesses can disappear quickly, but I personally believe that if you are confident in your product, your team and yourself, and you are always positive – working with sparkle, creativity and willingness – you can always succeed.

Over the years I have had to make and manage many changes. This is because the expectations of guests have changed a lot and so have the expectations and attitudes of staff. This means that, amongst other things, I have to change the ways I talk to both guests and staff. For example, with some guests now the best way to greet them is to say,

'Hi.' It is the language they use and so I use it too. Years ago, this would never have been the case in a 3 Michelin starred restaurant. Nowadays we have to be willing to adapt.

'The way I lead and motivate my team today,' he continues, 'is also different from how it used to be. The purpose of what I do does not change, only perhaps the language or my manner. Some of these changes are because of what I have learnt throughout my career. It is inevitable that many things change to a greater or lesser degree, so we have to change with them. Change is not a bad thing. Here we are always looking to create our own changes because we are always looking to improve. So you have the changes you make for yourself and the changes you make to keep up with the world. To stay at the top you need to do both. You can do this without changing your values or beliefs. This is a very important point! We do not change our beliefs about who we are, or about Service. We just change the way we express ourselves. We change some of the ways we please people. We never stop wanting to please.'

I am realising that one of the keys to longevity is to base what you do on a philosophy and principles that are, of themselves, timeless; to define your purpose in a way that guarantees its value regardless of the changes that occur around it. Whether Diego has done this deliberately from the very beginning is open to question. Yet in the final analysis it doesn't really matter because he has done it. He has built everything he does upon a foundation more enduring than the most powerful trend, a philosophy that is neither traditional nor current. That just simply *is*.

I write,

> Service is pleasing...It's timeless. Once you accept that this is, indeed, what Service is, you have committed yourself forever. *Serving is pleasing* becomes the moral to the story that you continually tell; you just adapt the contents to suit your current audience. The moral, however, stays the same. Serving is pleasing – always and forever.

I look up from my notebook and check my watch. I have only a few questions left and then we are finished. Diego knows too that we are getting towards the end. He waits patiently for me to continue.

'You haven't mentioned your competitors once,' I reflect. 'Why not?'

'To be honest with you, I am not competing against other businesses.' He raises both hands as he speaks. It is clearly not a gesture of surrender, more a sign that says, *Look I am hiding nothing*. He returns them to his lap and presses on. 'I am comfortable with what I do and what The Waterside Inn does. I am sure that many years ago I used to check the competition, but I have not done this for a long time.

Being comfortable does not mean that you become lazy. Rather that you believe in the value of what you are doing and are committed to always improving it.

What I do seems very natural to me. When something seems natural you don't think of competition; you just simply perform in a certain way because it feels right.'

His final comment brings together some of the key themes that have been running throughout this study. These are the relationship between nature and nurture, the importance of creating the right state from which to perform, and the pursuit of an ideal rather than simply competing against others.

Throughout Diego's professional career his employers and peers have acknowledged his innate instinct for Service. Yet despite his natural capabilities he has also actively pursued his own education, seeking out opportunities no matter how challenging from which to learn.

Now he is a committed trainer and mentor in his own right. He is proving that people with a passion and a desire to learn, even if they are not as innately gifted as he, can achieve excellence. He emphasizes both as a role model and through his training that attitude and state management are two powerful factors that influence, even determine, the quality of performance achieved.

His approach to competition turns the whole notion of gaining competitive advantage on its head. He isn't measuring the business performance of The Waterside Inn against others in the industry. He isn't interested in gaining an advantage over others. His focus is far more introverted than that. When he spends time thinking about and planning for the future it is only to ensure the continued financial success of the business he is committed to, to make it stronger.

At the very core of this is his never-ending journey to provide even better Service. If the search for the Holy Grail became a form of competition it was because men made it so, and by making it so they distracted themselves from the purity of their quest; they made it about themselves instead of *it*. Service defies such selfish attempts for glory, because Service is always about someone else.

The great and wonderful paradox is that Service really does influence the bottom line and, done well, it can be the source of business growth. However to provide the best Service you have to stop thinking about yourself, you have to forget any notion of winning, of rivalry, and give all of your attention instead to someone else. Power, it seems, lies in how skillfully you serve others, not in feelings of self-importance or authority.

According to many business theorists the number and quality of external relationships is another significant factor in determining how well a business does and for how long.

'How important is it that you have a strong network around you?'

'It is very important to have a healthy network around you. So, yes, I have a huge network. Guests are an important part of my network. I learn a lot from guests who are highly experienced in business, law, politics, the arts and so on. As we have discussed, I am a listener. I listen to everything and then I filter what I think is useful.

When staff leave they do so on good terms and I keep in touch with them. I am always here for them wherever they go and whatever careers they might move into. They are always there for me. We are there to help each other.'

'And they all know they can trust you?' I raise my inflexion at the end just to make it clear that I'm asking a question. We both know that it is rhetorical. He pretends that it isn't.

'Absolutely.' His eyes twinkle, hinting at a thousand hidden secrets. It would be impossible not to trust Diego.

The power of Service...

I hold the thought for a second or two. Then it is time to bring this, our final interview, to a close.

'Diego, can you provide your advice for staying at the top in just a few sentences?'

He inhales gently, his reply a soft and irresistible rat-a-tat-tat. 'My advice is to always be aware of what is going on around you and what is likely to be happening in the future. Always be on your guard. Honesty is a priority. Welcome guests with a genuine smile. Remember that, so far, a machine cannot replace a human being in providing great Service. Don't work with just your brain and your pocket, but also with your heart and your soul.'

He stops abruptly. His face lights up as it does when he is in the restaurant. He has a question of his own.

'Is that OK?' He asks.

I can't help but laugh. 'It's more than OK, Diego,' I say and we both sit back. 'It's more than OK.'

Summary

'Anyone can be great for a few days.'

The most significant challenge is not to achieve excellence, but to maintain it. This requires far more than just technical skill. It requires passion, creativity and the courage to adapt and change. It requires a powerful corporate identity, a philosophy and principles that are of timeless value, and remain constant even if the way they are expressed changes over time. Outstanding Service is essential for continued growth. Whilst the purpose of Service remains constant, the ways it is delivered needs to adapt to meet changing expectations.

The lessons are:

Lesson no. 1

Routines can dull the mind. They can kill creativity, enthusiasm and excitement. Leaders need to know when to be spontaneous, to create variety. They need to be willing to change routines and break rules. Spontaneity and variety help staff to think further than their feet. They encourage alertness. They create sparkle.

Lesson no. 2

You can please your guests *and* make a good profit. Turnover is not as important as profit; manage all costs carefully. Avoid waste. If possible train staff to multi-task. Always be looking for ways to maintain or improve standards whilst cutting costs. Be willing to offer something free to your guests. Such gifts tend to bring rewards at a later date.

Lesson no. 3

Service is the key to success. It creates repeat business. It creates positive word-of-mouth publicity. Guests who feel comfortable in your environment and with you are more likely to spend money. It is an error to treat guests differently according to how much they spend. Ensure that the red carpet is the same size for everyone.

Lesson no. 4

Build your business around your passion and your values. A central philosophy or value that is timeless provides the foundation for longevity. Live in the moment when serving guests; when thinking strategically identify the most likely future and plan to either manage or create it.

Lesson no. 5

The Devil is only in the detail if you fail to recognize, manage and continually improve those details. If, however, you manage all details well you will achieve on-going quality. There is always scope for improvement.

Lesson no. 6

Rest is essential. Change is inevitable. A powerful and positive network strengthens your position. Be alert to signs of fatigue within your staff; high-level performance cannot be maintained indefinitely. The quality of rest influences the quality of performance. Be alert to external changes and be willing to act accordingly. Be alert even – *especially* – when you are doing well. Build a network you can trust; if you serve it, it will also serve you.

∾

~

CONCLUSION

Finding yourself

~

'*The best way to find yourself is to lose yourself in the service of others.*'
Mahatma Gandhi

The philosophy, principles and practices of a Master of Service

Diego Masciaga lives to serve. He comes alive when he is pleasing others. He is a Master of his art. His example is a great reminder that we find ourselves only when we truly commit to what we believe in.

Through this study I have come to appreciate that Diego's work – his life – is based upon a philosophy that is translated through a number of guiding principles into a range of inter-related practices.

As we come towards the end it seems appropriate to offer the following brief discussion and summary:

Philosophy

Diego's philosophy can be condensed into three words,

Service is pleasing.

Yet there is much more. This is more than a philosophy for business success. This is the tip of a congruent, deeply held world-view.

Diego's philosophy is actually founded upon a profound understanding that Service is an inherent part of all relationships, formal and informal, corporate and social. How could it not be, given that it is the philosophy he learnt from his Mother?

Service, the Diego Masciaga way, is built on the belief that every Service interaction is a trust-based interaction. That whenever we give someone permission to serve us we are effectively saying, 'I trust you.'

Service, then, is a responsibility as well as a pleasure. And it *should be* a pleasure. When he says, 'Service begins with a genuine smile,' he is stating not only that a person should want to serve but that they should also enjoy the process of doing so. Philosophically, Diego views the act of Service as its own reward.

The more I consider his stance the more I find myself

reaching conclusions that I had neither expected nor considered at the beginning of my study. The corporate value of great Service is widely acknowledged. However, once I accepted Diego's premise that Service is pleasing, it was an easy next step to decide that Service is a central feature, even a responsibility, within all types of relationship. After all, we all want to please our family and friends, don't we? The truth is, sometimes we even go out of our way to please total strangers! Not only do we seek to please those we care about, we do so with a genuine smile.

So I find myself thinking, if Service is central to *all* relationships, and given that relationships are the myriad units and interactions that make up society, then it follows that Service is at the very centre of society. The quality of a society can be measured in no small part by the ways in which people *serve* each other.

This new line of thought creates a series of questions that I had not posed before. Questions I could ask of myself and others. Questions such as, 'Why have you developed your expertise and what do you intend to do with it?' 'Who do you serve?' Who do you know who you are *not* serving?' 'Why aren't you serving them?'

Whatever expertise or skills individuals develop it needs to be accompanied by at least a high level of Service ability. There is little value in having a skill set or a knowledge base that benefits others if you don't know how to provide and deliver it in ways that best serve their needs.

Service is pleasing.

It is one simple thing followed through completely. And once followed through it becomes both complex and powerful. Complex enough for it to fill Diego's life, to have made sense of who he is and what he does, and for perfection to have still eluded him. Powerful enough for him to have influenced many thousands of people, both professionals within and beyond his industry, and, of course, his many guests. Powerful enough to have built a global reputation for himself and the business he works for, and to have provided an immeasurable amount of pleasure.

Serving is pleasing is a philosophy with muscle. It is very hard work to serve brilliantly and consistently. It requires strength to make Service a living reality. It is a challenge and a dare, a risk and an opportunity wrapped up in the desire and willingness to assume responsibility for what someone else experiences and how this makes them feel.

It takes both courage and commitment to welcome customers into your business as you would welcome guests into your own home. Yet this is what Diego demands of his team and himself.

That is why he emphasises attitude over technique. Above all else, Service professionals have to want to please others. Ideally, they have to *need* to do it. They have to be willing to learn and develop the necessary skills, but even before they do that they have to understand with absolute clarity that Service creates its own power.

Acts of Service are neither weak nor demeaning. Service is Influence. Influence is inevitable. We influence others all the time, whether we mean to or not; whether we know it or not. The very best Service professionals influence deliberately and brilliantly. They reward our trust in them by meeting our personal needs in ways that make us feel that we are understood, valued and cared for. They make our interaction and our experience with them *sparkle*.

I can't now think of a business that doesn't need at least some brilliant Service professionals.

Diego's belief that *all* staff are involved in Service raises the bar – the challenge – even higher. His thinking in this regard is made up of two parts:

1) Service interactions are trust-based interactions and all staff, no matter what their role, have at least some colleagues who trust them to do certain things. Once someone places their trust in you, and you respect and respond to it, you are serving them.

2) Even if you do not interact with guests directly, you are an essential part of a professional chain that does create that direct interaction; you are serving your guests indirectly by serving the needs of those staff that do.

On a different level Diego demonstrates that leaders also serve. They serve a wide range of stakeholders including, for example, their staff, their guests, and their own boss.

He also demonstrates that a commitment to *Service is pleasing* does not mean always agreeing with others or even giving in to their demands. As a leader Diego knows when and how to say, 'No'. He says 'No' to his staff and criticises them as and when appropriate, but still he serves them by progressing their ability and their career. He knows that by doing this he is also serving the guests he might never meet who will one day be served by those he has influenced.

He also knows how to say 'No' to guests on those very rare occasions when it becomes necessary to do so. He does everything in his power to create a great experience for his guests until they become abusive and step over a line. At which point he chooses to please and protect those on his side of the divide.

Serving is pleasing is a philosophy with muscle, then, because it requires the courage to say 'No' as much is it requires the willingness to think further than your feet and so create a 'Yes' that exceeds expectation.

Diego's philosophy raises the question; shouldn't every business be based on a Service culture? It is a powerful, important question that demands our attention because:

1) It is a philosophy upon which he has created a most successful and enduring business.
2) It is widely accepted that outstanding Service creates repeat business and so fuels the bottom line.
3) It is equally accepted that poor Service damages the bottom line severely.

Yet it seems that so few businesses are truly committed to the challenge and rigour of delivering the very best Service they possibly can. Perhaps this is because they are unsure of how to go about it? Or it might be because they are confusing Service with the process of achieving an immediate sale? Perhaps for many the philosophy *Service is pleasing* has been corrupted into *Service is selling*? Or perhaps the notion of Service has been lost completely and been replaced by Selling?

For those wanting to develop the quality of the Service they provide, Diego has a framework of principles upon which he builds the Service he is famous for. They are applicable across industries and relate to the main areas covered in this book: recruitment; training; leadership; service delivery; longevity and consistency.

Principles

Diego's principles are the fundamental truths as he sees them of how to create outstanding Service. They combine to form a framework and a foundation for daily behaviours. It is his unrelenting adherence to these principles, the ways he unerringly translates them into every aspect of his role, that ensure the congruent, seamless approach I have sought to share with you. There are no gaps between what he thinks, says and does because he has tied these principles together so thoroughly there is no space for him to fall through.

They serve a far greater and more inspiring purpose than

just being his safety net, however. They combine to create the ideal to which Diego aspires. It is this ideal that, as I wrote at the beginning, keeps moving always just out of his reach. In this sense, his principles have a life of their own. They are dynamic and interactive, energising and elusive. They represent the sum of his understanding and yet, by having recognised them, he has also freed them to remain forever just out of his grasp in their perfect form.

The principles are:

Recruitment

- Excellence starts with recruitment.
- Recruit for attitude.
- Be uncompromising in your requirements when recruiting.
- Be creative; recruitment cannot be reduced to a universal process any more than Service can.

Training

- Train your staff formally and informally, little by little, day by day.
- Technique is the easiest thing to teach.
- Train staff to think like your thought leaders.
- Senior staff are role models; they must act accordingly.

Leadership

- Leadership is Service.
- Leaders need to be great storytellers.
- Leadership is dependent on trust.
- Loneliness is an inevitable part of leadership.
- Leaders are a part *of* the team; they are not *in* the team.
- Leaders need lieutenants, people who think like they do and share their vision.
- Leaders need to provide bespoke rewards as and when necessary to their staff.
- Leaders protect their staff from public criticism.
- Leaders need to be seen to be 100 per cent all of the time.

Service delivery

- Service means never having to ask.
- Service begins and ends with a genuine smile.
- Service is performance.
- Serve guests not customers.
- Everyone is a guest, even if they are not buying something today.
- Every guest is unique and should be treated as such.
- Outstanding Service is dependent upon the ability to determine and meet guests' individual needs continually.
- Serve from one step below.
- Too much Service is as bad as not enough.

- The guest is your guest until they leave, not until they pay.
- When a mistake happens, it is an opportunity to create something amazing.
- Thorough planning and preparation precedes the delivery of outstanding Service.
- The environment plays a vital role in Service delivery.
- Create the desired atmosphere and manage it continually.
- Every member of staff is involved either directly or indirectly in providing Service.
- Feedback is essential.
- Endings have to be brilliant.

Longevity and consistency

- Build your business around your passion and your values.
- Change routines and break rules.
- Spontaneity and variety help staff to think further than their feet.
- Turnover is not as important as profit.
- Avoid waste; manage all costs carefully.
- Be willing to offer something free to your guests. Such gifts tend to bring rewards at a later date.
- Comfortable guests are more likely to spend more money. Ensure, then, that your guests are comfortable with you and in your environment.
- Provide a red carpet that is the same size for everyone.
- Manage details rigorously; there is always scope for improvement.

- The quality of rest influences the quality of performance.
- Change is inevitable.
- Be alert for potential problems, especially when you are doing well.
- Build a network you can trust; if you serve it, it will also serve you.

Practices

From my observations Diego puts these principles into practice without conscious thought. They are such a part of his psyche and his purpose that he lives them and *pursues* them, continually. His example reminds me of the Four Stages of Learning model developed in the 1970s by Noel Burch that offered unconscious competence, the ability to perform at a high level easily as if by *second nature*, as the highest level. It could be argued that there is a fifth level – Mastery – at which a person is not only unconsciously competent but also understands precisely what they are doing and why and can share it with others.

Diego has achieved Mastery of his art. He assumes responsibility for recruitment and training. He is creative and flexible in his approach to recruitment. He tests applicants for attitude more than skill. He not only assumes responsibility for recruiting staff, but for helping them move on when the time is right for them to further their career. He merges recruitment, staff development and career progression in the seamless manner he does everything else. He creates great beginnings and even better endings for his staff just as he does his guests.

As the trainer and the leader, Diego operates as a deliberate and inspirational role model on a daily basis. He knows that when he is serving in the restaurant his staff are watching. He performs for them as well as he does those sitting at the tables.

He talks to all of his team every day. He uses their language and shares relevant stories. He repeats and reinforces key messages. He makes it clear that he understands them and he highlights what he and they have in common. He checks for signs of individual fatigue, providing additional time for rest and recuperation if he deems it necessary. He checks also for any signs of negativity and addresses these instantly and completely.

He uses the twice-daily briefing to maintain the sense of *team* and to ensure that everyone is ready to *sparkle*. He changes routines or creates problems for his team to solve, as ways of encouraging and developing creativity and teamwork.

He gives responsibility as a sign of trust. He rewards individuals in ways that he knows they will most appreciate. He ensures that he always honours the promises that he makes to them. He provides criticism at the time and in the place where he believes it will be best received, and he protects all of his staff from external critics.

He influences consistently and positively. He uses his authority to lead and motivate his team, to create commitment and consistency. He has developed and maintains a Service-based culture, a form of social proof that is compelling. He creates a sense of likeness and ensures that he is liked by staff and guests alike. He gives because he wants to and because he knows that most people will then give back, often in greater measure. He knows the value of scarcity and uses it.

Beyond all of this, Diego manages himself and his own standards. He varies his entrance every day, just to remind himself about the danger of routines and the need for him to see everything as if for the first time. He keeps his level of general knowledge high, so that he can engage with guests on their terms. He listens to and learns from his guests, regarding them as part of his network; a network that he manages with great care. He values and gives significant attention to his relationship with his boss, Michel Roux Snr. He gives as much attention to managing the finances as he does to understanding his guests.

In the restaurant, Diego takes responsibility for creating and/or managing the atmosphere. He leads by example. He demonstrates just why he is acknowledged globally as the Master of Service. There is no question his staff can ask of him that he cannot answer.

The final question

It ends as it began, in the summerhouse. Only this time we are sharing a conversation rather than an interview. We are creating closure.

The first time we sat here was nearly two years ago. I had so many questions to ask and as time passed that number grew. It grew because of Diego's openness and generosity of spirit, because he makes curiosity easy. It grew because he really is a Master and his answers often led me into rooms that I did not know existed within the great Hall of Service. Only Service isn't a building. It isn't even the greatest of great Halls. In many ways Service is far less obvious than a building, even though it has its own foundations and, just like buildings, it plays an essential role in the creation and maintenance of society.

No, Service is not a building. Because if it was I would have been able to resolve the one question I am going to take away with me unanswered. It is the one question I never asked. I wondered if I should. I considered it on several occasions. Every time I decided not to.

The question is the one that I asked myself early in our time together. The question is, 'What shape is Service?' I'm still convinced that everything must have a shape and if anyone knows the shape of Service it will be Diego.

But I'm not going to ask. Not even now, in our last few moments together. I'm not sure why. All I know is that it doesn't feel right. Maybe that's because I have reached that point where I know that I've asked enough, observed him for as long as anyone should be observed. That it is time, finally, to leave Diego alone. After all, he has given as freely and generously as anyone could. For the last two years I have been just one more person he has chosen to serve. And he has served me as well as he does his guests and his staff and his employer. The least I can do now is take my leave.

He walks me through the building to the reception. As he shakes my hand he thanks me for my time and my interest. He wishes me luck with my writing. He tells me that if I need any more information to just get in touch. He will always be available. It is his final lesson. I promise myself that I will find a way to show him my gratitude. He waits until our handshake is over before pursing his lips and frowning slightly. Then he leans in and whispers,

'You know, Mr. Parker, Service – it's a human thing.'

Yes, Diego. It is. I understand that now, far more than I ever did.

And then I realise that he has just answered my unasked question. Service excellence does not have a single shape. Service excellence is shaped in the moment by skilled professionals communicating with those who place their trust in them to best meet their needs. Service excellence is fluid and ever changing, the result of an interactive human process. Neither I nor anyone else can know its definitive shape because it doesn't have one.

I do know, however, where the many and varied Service-excellence shapes can be created. It is in the space between two people.

Knowing that is as good a starting point as any. After all, it's simple really. Service is a human thing.

That's why it matters so much.

~

AUTHOR BIOGRAPHIES

~

Chris Parker is a writer, presenter, management trainer and consultant. He lectures in Sport and Leisure Management at Nottingham Trent University and has taught on undergraduate and postgraduate programmes throughout the United Kingdom and Europe.

A specialist in interpersonal and intrapersonal communication, Chris has provided training for a wide range of personal and corporate clients and has written several books on communication and influence in business. He is the author of *Five Essential Ingredients for Business Success*; *Campaign It!* and the crime thriller *Influence*. All three titles are available on Amazon.

～

Diego Masciaga knows what it takes to run a successful restaurant. Having worked in the industry for over 30 years, his portfolio includes a stint at Le Gavroche, opening Le Mazarin in London (a restaurant which gained a Michelin star after four months) and he continues to make his mark at Michel and Alain Roux's Waterside Inn. The restaurant is the first outside of France to retain all three Michelin stars for over 30 years. Diego holds a Master of Culinary Arts, was awarded the Grand Prix de l'Art de la Salle from the L'Académie Internationale de Gastronomie in 2010. In 2011 Diego was awarded the title of Cavaliere, the Italian equivalent of a knighthood, for his commitment to the professional training and lifelong development of young people.

~

Urbane Publications is dedicated to developing new author voices, and publishing fiction and non-fiction that challenges, thrills and educates. From page-turning novels to innovative reference books, our goal is to publish what YOU want to read.

Find out more at
urbanepublications.com